THE RATIONAL MALE

VOLUME II

PREVENTIVE MEDICINE

ROLLO TOMASSI

The Rational Male • Volume II – Preventive Medicine, first edition copyright © 2015 Rollo Tomassi.

ISBN-13: 978-1508596554
ISBN-10: 1508596557

Published by Counterflow Media LLC, Reno, Nevada
Design and layout by Rollo Tomassi.

CONTENTS

FORWARD
By Sam Botta

INTRODUCTION

BOOK I

CONTENTS

BOOK II
SUPPORT WORKS

This book is dedicated to the memories of the 22 American veterans who take their own lives every day in 2015

FORWARD

"Where were you, Rollo Tomassi, when I was 18, 33, 42?"

"Hey Sam, it's over, you've lost frame. In other words, Sam, she's checked out of the relationship because she sees you as needy."

Ouch!

Wait a minute! All these years I'm paid to sound like the *Man*, I interview the A-list at The Oscars, I'm invited to the after parties, my life is fun, billionaires regularly meet with me to pick my brain, women find me attractive, I'm unusually successful and I'm on the list everywhere, so how could this happen to me? Because of choices made in my line of work, I was immune to a woman checking out of a relationship like that since I'm an outlier, right?

Rollo would say "It's about Sexual Market Value Sam. You went from being an outlier because of notoriety, to a man on your back in inpatient care. You stopped acting like that Man, so she sees you like a girlfriend that she doesn't even like."

The Rational Male explained what I and millions of other men do and have done to cause a woman that once had genuine desire for us to check out of the relationship… and what to do about it.

This book is contains that knowledge and wisdom. It's THAT powerful.

I'm that voice you've heard a thousand times. Movies, trailers, radio spots. In all my years as a voice actor, I've never read anyone's work that sounded like my movie trailer voice, until I read the first essays at therationalmale.com.

The words of Tomassi felt like I feel when I'm putting myself into the script because that's how to change the course of world events through a blockbuster film.

I know of no one that's read *The Rational Male* who isn't transformed by it. If someone has handed this book to you, that person is loyal to you and loves you. It's real. Never forget that.

This book is going to transform everything in your life into a better state.

In our times too many men are committing suicide because the woman he loves has lost her genuine desire for him. This book is the quintessential work that has it all, it's the full experience that's been proven to prevent those suicides.

It's not a motivational seminar, it's not a meditation retreat, it's simple truth mined from almost 15 years of observations and deep discussions among millions of men.

You've heard those people say that they can't wait until they get on the other side so they can have all their questions answered. Forget that. This powerful resource has answers like that... answers that have been intentionally hidden from you through all of your education, entertainment, family, friends and life.

Know this now: You are going to be bothered by some of what you read. You're a man, you can deal with it. You're A Man. You will deal with it.

The concepts in it are so powerful, I challenge you to complete this book within three days. Then, read it again, slowly.

I have this book my Uncle gave me while I was in college. He's passed away now, but I still carry that little book *I Dare You* first published 90 years ago by *William H. Danforth*. I carry it with me wherever I go. *The Rational Male* is like that.

He doesn't write for money. He's doing this to make the world a better place to live. He's writes because he wants you to make the most of yourself. Though he could afford a major marketing and branding campaign, nothing has been spent on either. It all started with helping one person, now, through his blog and his first book, more than seven million have experienced the kind of change that enhances every aspect of life. There is no doubt that you'll become as obsessed with absorbing this material - and spreading it - as I am.

I'm honored to have been asked to write this forward. This material has changed the course of my life. My 'nice guy' ways needed something more. Success, status may attract her, but without a guide, without a map, there's no way 99% of men will continue to spark her genuine desire.

It's worked for me and for everyone I've introduced to it. It's saved me from further heartbreak in life from relationships with women. Married men tell me the nightmares in their lives with wives that no longer see the value in emotional connection through the wonder of sexual intercourse. I tell them that would be misery, and I refer them to the work of Rollo Tomassi.

This book is written by a man that's become a close friend. I admire him like I admire my heart transplant surgeon brother. My brother has such precise mastery of his art that heart surgeons around the world utilize new techniques he discovered. When most surgeons follow his lead, more lives are saved each year. Rollo Tomassi has such mastery of his art that it's improving the lives of millions of people around the world.

He's personally counseled me for free, and to men that are sincerely trying to learn the truths and wisdom he writes about, he counsels them for free as well. And this advice isn't the standard advice that will cause you to further damage your relationship with that special someone. This advice works. I'm living proof.

I've enjoyed the benefits of unusual success. My work has influenced the lives and habits of millions of people each year. Through all of it, I've realized that the work I do using an alias gives people what they want, and some things that people want may not be best for them. So my sharing this book with you is also a way for me to make up for the influence some of my work has spread during my career. Rollo Tomassi is the only author I know who's unplugging men from "The Matrix" effectively.

Why does Rollo Tomassi not use his real name? The material is simply too powerful, and that can be dangerous. As I've stated, I'm known for parts of my work, but certainly not all of it. None of it is immoral, it's just that the spotlight would be too bright if the world knew.

I was in college, walking with a few sorority girls that were talking about how this other guy was a jerk and why couldn't he be a nice guy. I said, "I'm a nice guy," and they all laughed. I didn't understand that because I was reared to be nice.

Have you ever been blindsided by a break-up, then, the next time someone broke up with you, you wanted answers.

When I found Rational Male, I had been blindsided by another breakup. I wasn't going to go to a PUA (Pick Up Artist) seminars, and anything you could buy as a book had advice that was mainly about getting in touch with my feminine side. No matter what success I've had, I could never "just get it" when it came to keeping a woman attracted in a long-term relationship.

I get it now.

Sam Botta
Voice Actor, Radio Personality
Burbank, California – 2015

Introduction

At the time of my writing this volume my first book, The Rational Male, is less than a year old. It was certainly an effort in experimentation to say the least. There were a lot of issues I hadn't foreseen – font size issues, editing and grammatical issues, conversion to a digital format (twice) – and that was just with the book itself. I had severely underestimated the popularity of a digital format, and how most readers enjoy a book on their eReaders, especially in countries where an Amazon printed copy was hard to come by.

Despite all of these issues, and in under a year, The Rational Male has become a success. Not because it increased the readership and popularity of the blog, nor because it's still selling briskly, but because it has accomplished what I'd hoped it would.

I had hoped to reach a broader readership by putting these ideas, literally, into the hands of men who would otherwise dismiss them from a blog link. I wanted something tangible for men (and women) to share with other men. I purposely kept it as affordable as Amazon would allow so the book might be carried into a coffee house or on an airplane, where hopefully the title would spark a discussion – even if just from scoffing at the title.

I'm often asked why I put so much effort into the printed version, particularly since the digital sales regularly exceed those of the printed book. I'll admit that my artistic sense and design background had a need to be satisfied, but I wanted a book for the 'everyman' – one that a guy working in a garage might find accessible, or one a soldier deployed in a very unfamiliar, inhospitable place might take along with him.

You can't delete a book. You can burn a book, shred it or otherwise physically destroy that book, but you have to take it into your hands to do so. As melo-dramatic as this sounds, I fear that there may be a day when the authorities of digital publishing will become the authorities of permissible information. Deleting a book would be as simple as a keystroke.

I had actually intended this volume to be a standalone digital format book, however my sense of aesthetics, and a small bit of wanting to hold another book in my own hands won out. Of course there is a digital version to make it accessible, you may even be reading it now, but bear in mind that books and the ideas contained within are meant to be discussed – or at least that's how I'd intend these ideas.

Terminologies

In The Rational Male I presented the core concepts of what I consider *Red Pill Thought*. A lot of people in, and familiar with, the collectively male blog-space known as the 'manosphere' understand what "the red pill" is – a euphemism, courtesy of the Matrix movies, for a revelation of truth in a system that's kept them blind to that truth.

For most people with fresh eyes to the manosphere this sounds exactly like the schlock they've come to expect from online communities. Using movie references, in-group jingoisms, and cryptic acronyms seems par for the course, but it's important to remember that new concepts demand new terminologies.

It's kind of hard to ask a new reader to try and read past these terms for the first time. A common complaint is a lack of reference for these terms or acronyms, and in the interests of helping the fresh eyes I've included an appendix of sorts at the end of the book to accommodate these new readers. That said, it's important to bear in mind that terms, references and acronyms serve the purpose of labeling and outlining more broad or abstract concepts.

For instance one large point of contention most men unfamiliar with the manosphere or Red Pill thought chafe against is the concept, and categorization, of Alpha and Beta men. I dedicated a long section of The Rational Male to outlining and defining *my* interpretation of what constitutes the characteristics of both these types of men, and predictably, it often confuses or angers men's ego-protection instinct. And just as predictably, an otherwise productive discussion of a broader idea becomes mired in an endless (sometimes hopeless) defining of mutually acceptable terms.

In this volume of Rational Male, bear in mind that terms 'Alpha' or 'Beta' or any other term you might find esoteric are meant to be placeholders for abstract concepts. While I've attempted to minimize the manosphere-specific references and jingoism, there will still be instances of core concepts that are just simpler to describe in terms of 'Alpha' or 'Beta' in order to outline a larger dynamic – or in this book's case, how a man will be categorized by women at specific phases of her (and his own) maturation.

So, I humbly ask that any new reader struggling with these terms for the first time refer to The Rational Male for more specific definitions. This volume will presume you're familiar with the ideas I put forth in The Rational Male, so consider this book an accompaniment to the core concepts therein.

Why I wrote this book

Around mid-March of 2014 I endeavored to write a series of articles called Preventative Medicine on the Rational Male blog. I did so with the hope of providing my readers with a chronological outline of what to expect from women at various phases of women's maturation throughout their lives. Consequently, this series was prompted by a 2010 article posted on the Château Heartiste blog titled *The Difficulty Of Gaming Women By Age Bracket*. In that post *Roissy* breaks down the pick-up artistry involved in using Game at various phases of women's lives and how best to capitalize on what can usually be expected of western(ized) women.

I had read this post when it was first published and bookmarked it. It seemed like a seminal post from Roissy at the time and I've referenced it in various posts on my own blog occasionally. However, as I kept referring back to it I never really made the connection as to how women's lives (and by association men's lives) tended to follow a somewhat predictable series of phases. For a pick up artist, interested in maximizing his lay-count, the utility of knowing what to expect from a woman in a certain age demographic, culture (or subculture) and socioeconomic tier is fairly obvious – know your quarry, adapt your approach.

Something clicked for me after referring back to this article so often when I was doing consults for various men seeking advice about a specific woman and the circumstances they found themselves dealing with. As ever, one of the most common regrets (if that's the word) men relate to me is that they wish they'd had the information I've offered in The Rational Male and on the blog when they were younger so as to have avoided some debilitating, life-affecting decision with a woman. It's usually either that or some regret about the present situation they find themselves in and how horrible and regrettable the truth of the Red Pill has been for them.

It occurred to me that a more expanded version of a *'what to expect with a woman at this age'* post might be in order. This then developed into the four part series of Preventative Medicine articles, as well as being the inspiration for more than a few follow-up posts that further expanded understanding the "time line" of women's life progressions.

The problem I ran into was that providing such an exhaustive outline for my online readership tends to be a test of their attention spans. I think one of the biggest obstacles to really understanding a blog post's point is the 'tl;dr' phenomenon – "too long; didn't read."

This wall-of-text a commenter painstakingly typed out may be a hidden gem of philosophical brilliance, but in one swift 'tl;dr' act of desperation all that brilliance is distilled to a plea to a readers internet attention deficit disorder by summing it up in an easily digestible info-bite at the end.

So, in order to avoid overloading my readers with too much at once, it seemed like the best idea would be to break this progression down into a series of four (albeit long) posts to cover the 'points of interest' adequately.

The reader response to this series exceeded anything I could've foreseen.

To say the comments were insightful would be an understatement. Many different perspectives were expressed, but all had more to add to the progression and all made an attempt to address some particular aspect of the progression (and what men might expect at that point in the progression) that they felt was vital to a full understanding of women at various stages of maturity.

I had men in every demographic adding their understanding to the collective purpose of providing other men with what they've experienced and what to possibly expect at that phase of life. Young men of 18 would relate their frustrations with having to deal with breakups after graduating high school and being torn between going to a university they thought was best for them or transferring to the school their 'soul mate' high school girlfriend was going to attend in order to maintain (or rescue) the relationship.

Alternatively, I had men in their mid-sixties relate stories about the circumstances that led to their divorces and the issues they'd experienced in dealing with their ex-wives and the older (and younger) women they were dating at a time of their lives in which they never thought they'd be dating again.

After the second installment of this series one of my regular readers and Christian-manosphere blogger, Donalgraeme commented the following:

"Its amazing, when you consider it, to think of the various social constructs/conventions built up to support this female model of development. At each and every stage there are a slew of different organizations and support sources which encourage women along every step of the path. It would be a good thing to map them out, actually. You know, to peg different sources to different time periods in the 'life-path.' Starting from Teen magazines and the Disney channel all the way to various middle-age celebrity and gossip mags."

This planted the germ of the idea that's developed into the book you now hold in your hands.

So it's with this in mind that I set out to detail as best I could a chronological *time line* in which men might be better prepared to understand and develop ways to deal with the particulars a woman would be experiencing at various phases of her life.

Furthermore, I've endeavored to a marginal degree to account for outlying variables and experiences that may modify the more predictable aspects of women's phases of life. Obviously I couldn't exhaustively account for every circumstance, but I've attempted to address how the most common decision women make at these various stages affect the later phases, and then how men might best prepare contingencies for, or avoid entirely, the consequences of associating with the women making those decisions.

This *time line* wouldn't be complete unless I also factored in the social conventions erected around each of these phases and how they modify, affirm or attempt to absolve the personal and social ramifications implicit to each phase. As such I've addressed the most common social conventions men might expect to encounter during these phases of women's maturation.

I'll point out now that my individual effort to make this time line is in no way intended to be comprehensive. I wouldn't presume to be so thorough in my scope here to think I'm going to cover every aspect of this maturation process – I'm simply providing you with my best estimate as drawn from my own experiences and those of the men who've shared theirs with me over the course of my time writing in the manosphere.

As with the first Rational Male book, I ask that you understand I'm a connector of dots – I leave it to my readers to see the bigger picture.

I expect most men reading this work will disagree with certain aspects of my outlines of these phases as they apply to their own circumstances with the women they interact with personally. Some phases may not seem relevant to a particular phase men find themselves in presently, but may be relevant in their future.

Other men will likely nod in ascension or shake their heads knowingly when I cover a phase they've experienced personally. For all these men, understand that my purpose, as with all my writing, is to better inform men what they might expect at various phases of their own lives, why those expectations are likely and how best to prepare accordingly for them.

How to read this book

In the introduction of The Rational Male I made mention of a reader, Jacquie, who's son she said was in need of being made aware of the ideas I'd written about online for over a decade. The point being her hope was that what I'd written might help him avoid bad life decisions based on his unfortunate, feminine-conditioned mindset.

My intent is much the same for this book as well, however, I've tried to be more comprehensive in outlining situations that apply to women at significant stages of their maturity. In doing so my intent for men is to help them not to simply avoid making bad future decisions, but to aid them in understanding what they've experienced up to the point of their particular circumstances with women in the now.

The purpose of this book is to help you better understand the circumstances of what's led up to whatever part of this time line you find yourself on, what you're currently experiencing with a woman (or potential women) and what you might expect from women at future points of their maturation.

The Time Line

The first thing you'll be aware of is the time line graph I've established to help you get a visual grasp of various phases of women's maturity. At certain points along this time line I detail what I believe are the most prominent periods of situational change, crisis, personal insight (both convenient and genuine) and the psychological and belief changes women most commonly pass through.

Also along this graph I've placed sub-periods of how I believe women prioritize the importance of what they find attractive, arousing and generally filter for in men during different parts of their maturation. Though this aspect of the time line has definite (Game) applications for men in adjusting how they might best appeal to women in these phases, my purpose in adding these sub-periods is to illustrate the 'hows' and the 'whys' that motivate many of the decisions women are prone to make during these phases.

I've broken the time line down into four sections in four corresponding chapters; late adolescence through early adulthood, early twenties through early thirties, mid-life, and later life.

The temptation of course will be for readers to skip ahead to phases a man might be currently experiencing at his own point of personal circumstance, but I'll urge you to read the chapters in order. Your understanding of a particular personal crisis, or why you might be enjoying a better relationship earlier or later in life, are more or less contingent upon the general path a woman might take during her maturation to get to the point you're experiencing now.

By all means, go back and re-read certain sections later, but getting a general understanding of the maturation process, and what may or may not apply to a particular personal situation is necessary first.

The Sexual Market Value Graph

Many of the significant periods I detail in the time line also correspond with my now infamous sexual market value (SMV) graph. I introduced this *very generalized* graph in The Rational Male in the chapter, *Navigating the SMP* (sexual marketplace). I've included it in this volume as well for convenience sake as I refer to it to illustrate certain points in women's maturation. If you haven't read this particular chapter from the first book I'd encourage you to do so as it will help your understanding of those references.

Social Conventions

Following the outline of each phase of maturity, I'll cover what I've found to be the most common social conventions a feminine-primary social order has established to justify, affirm or excuse the experiences and decisions women make during these phases – as well as to be used to condition men to be accommodating of that feminine-primacy.

While each phase has operative social conventions unique to that stage of a woman's maturity, there are some which span several. Furthermore, some conventions affect the consequences, outcomes or even the likely occurrence of women subscribing to other conventions that follow from an earlier originating convention.

Needless to say accounting for every eventuality that comes from these conventions is not really feasible to outline, but the overall progression of those conventions is the important point. With a good overview men will have the tools to better grasp the progression of conventions, and the present convention, that color and influence the circumstances of a particular woman at her phase of maturity.

Outliers

In the interests of being as thorough as I can I've added some considerations for what I refer to as *outliers* at various parts of each section. These end notes are meant to account for some of the more common outlying personal situations which women may experience that, for whatever reason, may disqualify women from following the more predictable paths a certain phase of maturity will generally predispose most women to.

In most instances these outliers don't change a woman's larger experience of the phase of maturity, but the outlying circumstances and decisions a woman makes often modify the progression.

In addition, these outliers also create or modify social conventions to accommodate, affirm (often with male participation) and absolve the consequences of the decisions women make as a result of those outlying circumstances.

Book II – Supporting Chapters

Finally, I've added several supporting chapters I hope will answer some of the more common questions and issues that will inevitably follow for certain, significant phases of this time line. Most of these topics originated as follow-up posts on The Rational Male blog, but I've reviewed and reconsidered many aspects of those posts and felt they deserved a greater mention in the whole of this work.

Many of these support chapters directly reflect or help explain the various dynamics of a particular phase, while others present a broader perspective that may span several, or sometimes all, phases of maturation. I selected these particular sections with the consideration that they serve a cautionary or informative purpose that will help men to grasp the larger aspects of the time line itself.

I've included most of this support in the second half of the book (Book II), but I've begun with the chapter *Understanding Hypergamy* because I feel this very base-nature dynamic serves as the cornerstone for every man to really come to terms with feminine nature.

It is my sincere hope that this work will benefit your personal situation and interactions with the same impact and gravity that The Rational Male provided men with. As I began in the first book, I consider myself a connector of dots; and for the most part I always make an earnest attempt to present my ideas in as honest an observation as I'm able.

So once again I'll stress that The Rational Male – Preventive Medicine is not intended to be the final, definitive word on any of the issues or phases you'll read hereafter. This volume is not intended to be comprehensive, but rather an outline to prompt even further discussion and understanding of these phases of maturity.

As with everything I write, you'll likely grate against and disagree with various aspects of what I describe, and later some aspect will resonate so strongly with you that you'll only be able to shake your head at yourself for not having considered it in the same light when you first experienced that aspect with a woman at that phase of maturity.

This *is* the intent of this book. I want you to be angry. I want you to nod in agreement and shake your head when you don't. I want you have questions and I certainly want you to consider the validity of what you're about to read and how they apply to your past, present and future interactions with women – as well as how they might apply to men you know or are related to who have yet to experience them.

It's only preventive medicine if you can pass along the warning.

I'm always flattered when readers think I'm some phenomenal interpreter of psychology, the nature of women, intergender relations and a model upon which men should aspire to in order to get laid and still have a great (now 18 year) marriage. I honestly wish I was that guy, but that's not Rollo Tomassi.

I'm a student of life just as much as you likely are, and as such I understand the value of knowing that I *know* nothing really. These are my observations. They are not cannon, they are not law. So with this in mind I ask again in this book that you read with an open mind and with any luck we'll both become better men (and women) for the time you consider these observations.

As always, I'm as accessible as a comment on The Rational Male blog or a quick email (on my *About* page) if you have any questions or maybe a consideration you think I haven't considered.

Rollo Tomassi
February 2015

BOOK I

"Why do my eyes hurt?"

"You've never used them before."

UNDERSTANDING HYPERGAMY

YOUR FRIEND MENSTRUATION

There are methods and social contrivances women have used for centuries to ensure that the best male's genes are selected and secured with the best male provisioning she's subjectively capable of attracting. Ideally the best Man should exemplify the best of both aspects, but rarely do the two exist in the same male (particularly these days), so in the interest of achieving her biological imperative, and prompted by an innate need for security, the feminine as a whole needed to develop social conventions and methodologies (which change as her environment and personal conditions do) to effect optimizing women's innate Hypergamy.

Years ago, when I was writing the post that would become the *Schedules of Mating* chapter of my first book, my emphasis was on how an evolved dynamic (female pluralistic sexual strategy) translated into evolved social dynamics (feminine primary social conventions). My focus then was on how the feminine creates and normalizes social conditions that favor Hypergamy by covertly manipulating social expectations – not only of the men who would optimize that Hypergamy, but also for women themselves in how their own self-rationalizations (hind-brain, hamsters) can be socially justified.

I wrote the post *Schedules of Mating* in 2005 (on SoSuave) in an effort to explain the rudiments of Hypergamy in a more accessible way for guys who were still struggling with understanding why women would say they wanted "a Nice guy with a good heart" yet would, in stark contradiction of this, behaviorally opt for Bad Boy-Jerks as their sexual partners of choice. I still think it's a pretty good essay, which is why I revised and included it in the earliest posts at Rational Male. However, even at the time I was writing, I knew that the concept of an evolved Hypergamy and its social implication still had a lot more under the hood to explore.

Biological Hypergamy

The following is a quote from a 2008 study on hormones and brain activity from the *Kinsey Institute.*

"One area of the brain in which we observed a difference in activation in response to masculinized versus feminized faces — specifically during the follicular phase — was the anterior cingulate cortex, which is a region involved in decision-making and the evaluation of potential reward and risk," said neuroscientist Heather Rupp, research fellow at the Kinsey Institute for Research in Sex, Gender and Reproduction. "Activation in this region has been previously reported to correlate with 'high risk' nonsocial choices, specifically monetary risk, so it is interesting that it is observed to be more active in response to masculinized male faces, who may be both riskier but more rewarding to women."

There are a multitude of studies that indicate women's sexual preference for facial characteristics shift depending on their menstrual phase. These fluctuating preferences are thought to reflect evolutionarily founded changes in women's reproductive priorities.

Around the time of ovulation women prefer more masculinized faces — faces with features that indicate high levels of testosterone. These facial cues predict high genetic quality in the male because only such males can afford the immune system-compromising effects of testosterone. Testosterone may be costly for the males' mates as well because high testosterone levels also are associated with high rates of offspring abandonment.

Around the time of ovulation, a female's preference apparently shifts from avoiding negligent parenting to acquiring the best genes for her offspring. This principle is known in evolutionary psychology as *Ovulatory Shift*.

At other points during the cycle, women will prefer more feminized male faces, as they might signal a higher willingness of the males to invest in offspring.

If you'll pardon the vernacular, what Ovulatory Shift represents in a social context is what's known in the manosphere as the Alpha Fucks and Beta Bucks principle; the drive for an optimization between the best direct genetic benefit (sex) and the best indirect benefit (parental investment and provisioning) is a biologically hard-wired feature of the female mind.

Studies like this aren't unknown to the manosphere, and even the early Pickup Artist (PUA) teachers had an almost instinctual understanding of how a woman's ovulatory cycle could affect a guy's odds of a successful hookup without ever having read them. Needless to say, there's a plethora of practical applications a man might develop with a firm knowledge of how a woman's hormonal cycle affects her mood, her susceptibility to his influence and how her post-sex ratio-

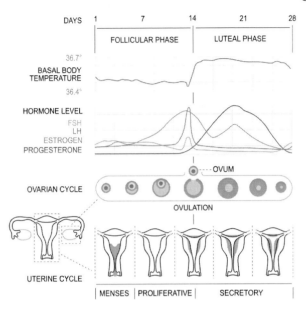

DAYS 1 7 14 21 28

FOLLICULAR PHASE | LUTEAL PHASE

36.7°
BASAL BODY TEMPERATURE
36.4°

HORMONE LEVEL
FSH
LH
ESTROGEN
PROGESTERONE

OVUM

OVARIAN CYCLE

OVULATION

UTERINE CYCLE

| MENSES | PROLIFERATIVE | SECRETORY |

nalization will be altered as a result of the particular phase of her menstrual cycle she happens to be in.

In his Blue Pill years, I think a lot of what accounts for a guy's sporadic successes with women can be attributed to the woman's ovulatory phase and favorable circumstance. Right phase, right place, right time and a guy who gave off just enough subconscious masculine prompts and Alpha cues to get the lay – or the brief girlfriend status until her subsequent follicular phase peaked and he wasn't the 'Alpha' she thought he was three weeks prior.

The Alpha Phase

From a Game perspective, using the above illustration as a guide, the latter half of the follicular (proliferative) phase – the period between day 7 to about day 14 – might be called the Alpha Phase for Men. The Kinsey study (and many similar ones) would indicate that this 7 (maybe 10) day window predisposes women to (Alpha) masculinized sexual influence and would be the optimal period for a man to make a lasting Alpha impression. Sexual tingles are most commonly born in the proliferative phase.

It's during this phase women are more predisposed to sexual ornamentation (dressing sexy) and vocal intonation changes, masculine body odor becomes more appealing and an overall preference for masculinized physical attributes (muscularity) intensifies as arousal cues for her in men. Female biochemistry and its resultant behavior patterns *shift* in the proliferative phase to optimize breeding potential with the 'Best Genes' (direct benefit) male a woman has, or makes available to herself by subconscious design.

I've caught a lot of grief in the past from angry women for suggesting that all women have an 'inner slut', and that all a guy need do is be the right man at the right time to bring this out in them. An understanding of the behavioral changes of Ovulatory Shift during women's menstrual cycle puts a punctuation on this.

The hot coed on spring break in Cancun who fucks the cute guy in the foam cannon party is most likely in her proliferative phase. Add alcohol and you've got the chemical formula for sexual urgency – even from the 'good girl'.

When she thinks or says "I don't know what came over me, I'm not usually like this" she's observing her proliferative phase behavior from a luteal phase perspective. She really isn't "like that" the other 21 days of her cycle.

It's during this part of a woman's cycle that she become subconsciously attuned to masculinized traits and makes subliminal efforts to capitalize on her concurrent ovulation. In other words, this is the period in which *Hypergamy doesn't care* the most. It's "fuck me now, I'll rationalize it out later."

About now you're probably wondering, "That's all well and good, but how do I determine what cycle phase a woman is in?"

If all a guy were doing was cold approaches with women I could understand the confusion. There are countless 'tells' women will display when they are in their proliferative phase.

Dr. Martie Hasselton of UCLA has done some excellent studies on female ornamentation coinciding with ovulation and also how women's vocal pitch shifts lower (sultry voice) during this phase, but if you're still unconvinced, listen to your gut – men instinctually know when women are in the pro phase of ovulation. In fact, the phenomenon of 'Mate Guarding' is a well studied dynamic that appears to have evolved in men as a result of a subconscious awareness of women's behavioral cues during the period of their ovulation.

If you have the patience to learn, pay better attention to the behaviors of the women in your immediate social circle, or to the behaviors of the girl you think you may want to target at some point.

Beta Phase

If the proliferate phase is the Alpha Phase for Men, then the luteal phase could be considered the Beta Phase.

Again using the Kinsey study, as well as many from *Dr. Hasselton* as our general guide we can infer that women become drawn to more feminine features in men during the 14 day down side of their cycle. The attributes of attraction (not arousal) that define this stage are associated with comfort, familiarity, empathy, nurturing, etc. meant to reinforce the perception that a man is a good choice for long-term parental investment.

Again, this is nothing novel in the manosphere. Even my manosphere colleague, Roissy has written several posts regarding the applied use of Beta-side Game – within context. Far too many men believe the WYSIWYG (what you see is what you get) myth about women and their advertised attraction requisites as being predominantly Beta-associative.

As I illustrated before, the girl who spontaneously banged the hot guy in the foam cannon party is the same girl who'll say you need to earn her trust because she needs to be comfortable with you before you have sex. Beta-prone men believe this at face value and don't strike while the iron's hot (the proliferate phase), wait her out and wonder why they get a, "lets just be friends" at the end of her luteal phase.

I think where most Beta men lose the trail is in the belief that Beta attraction is (or should be) synonymous with Alpha arousal. Each of these concepts is representative of a different facet of women's pluralistic sexual strategy – Hypergamy – Alpha seed, Beta need. Women's sexual imperatives can be defined by the degree to which her short term mating strategy can be justified, or offset, by her long term mating strategy.

Nowhere is this disparity more obviously manifested than in the biological reality of a woman's menstrual cycle which creates it.

The Hypergamy Link

One aspect of Hypergamy that I'm not certain most men really understand is that the socio-sexual strategy that is Hypergamy is a biological phenomenon in origin.

To fully understand the time line I present in this book, it's important not to confuse Hypergamy with being a social construct (i.e. "marrying up").

Women almost categorically, even deliberately, maintain a strict definition of Hypergamy as only a learned social dynamic. This is more from a need to protect the rationalizations that result from confronting the uncomfortable internal conflict that Hypergamy causes for them. You'll hear women agonize with themselves, "why am I not hot for the sweet Beta who'd give me the world, but cannot get enough sex from the hot guy who's casually indifferent to me?"

The Feminine-Primary Social Order

The base truth of Hypergamy as a social dynamic is that it is the logical result of women's innate, hormonal and psychological firmware. This root-level disparity of a dualistic sexual strategy (Alpha Fucks / Beta Bucks) led to the evolution of the feminine psyche – to be covert, to be excusably duplicitous, an evolved psychological capacity to be better communicators on more varied levels, but also to be the nurturers necessary to raise the next generation. Without this facility for being beneficially duplicitous on a psychological level, women cannot as effectively optimize their sexual strategy.

Since the sexual revolution began, the biological rationale for social feminization has been men's biological proclivity for violence and aggression. Our biological proclivities make us potentially dangerous. We're told that we're poisoned by our testosterone; we're controlled from youth to repress that in school to the point where teachers expect boys to 'act out', so we drug them.

Yet, the biological rationale for Hypergamy could also be said to lie in women's biological (menstrual) impetus that motivates their sexual pluralism. It is exactly this biological motivation which a feminine-primary social order has been established in the wake of the sexual revolution.

As you read through the following time line it's important to fully grasp the feminine-primary motivators behind the reasonings for the personal and social shifts a woman will experience at various phases of her maturity.

Understanding Hypergamy

The reason I'm beginning with Hypergamy before we get too involved in this chronology is because it's important to get a good idea of Hypergamy's incentives and how they motivate women during these phases.

The social aspect and the personal aspect of women's maturation process hinges upon how Hypergamy influences women's decision making – and ultimately affects the men who engage with them during those phases of her life.

Both the personal and social elements of Hypergamy work in concert to produce a relatively predictable chain of events, personal crises and life decisions throughout a woman's life.

Much of the manosphere likes to define Hypergamy as a woman getting the best bang for her attractiveness buck, but this is only one side of Hypergamy.

Using the Alpha Fucks / Beta Bucks principle of women's dualistic sexual strategy it becomes clear that there is a drive to balance Hypergamy between these two impulses. As I began in *Schedules of Mating*, Hypergamy wants to have both sides of a woman's sexual strategy equation satisfied by the same man, but rarely is this dualistic satisfaction met in the same individual, and increasingly more men are becoming aware of this strategy.

It's my belief that a drive for hypergamic optimization exists in both the impulse to secure the best genes (sexy son theory – Alpha Fucks) and the best provisioning / emotional investment (parental investment – Beta Bucks) a woman's attractiveness can be leveraged for.

The problem then is one of leveraging her attractiveness relative to any particular phase of her life and the circumstance that phase dictates for her. Needless to say a woman's physical conditions, her personal decisions and modern social pressures will influence this 'balancing act' (careerism, feminism, religious conviction, etc.), but it's only half correct to apply Hypergamy only to the Alpha Fucks side of women's dualistic sexual strategy.

Finally, it's also important to consider that, from an evolutionary standpoint, Hypergamy always seeks an optimization of either side of the AF/BB motives that is *better,* more advantageous, than any individual woman's attractiveness should realistically warrant. Hypergamy doesn't seek its own level, it will always seek a better optimization than a woman's sexual market value has a realistic expectation to afford her.

Also keep in mind that modern social pressures (social media etc.) exacerbate this, and further distort women's realistic evaluations of their own sexual market value (SMV) at any given phase of her life. The most secure, monogamous attachments women will make are with Men they perceive to be 1 to 2 points above what she perceives is her own relative SMV.

I had a Rational Male reader pose the following question on the blog:

> *Knowing what we know about Hypergamy – that it's inborn and does not give a crap – and also what we know about women's attraction cues swaying toward much more Alpha men during ovulation…can men deal with the thought of living with someone who is having to fight against (presuming she's fighting against it) a general innate desire to trade up and a specific desire to stray with an Alpha male during ovulation?*

The short answer to this is yes, in fact men have had socially and psychologically evolved contingencies to mitigate Hypergamy since our hunter-gatherer beginnings. You could even argue that much of our cultural and species-level achievements were the result of men's latent drives to deal with women's innate Hypergamy.

The common mistake is to presume that Hypergamy's natural state exists in a vacuum. Hypergamy is not static. The capacity an individual woman possesses to optimize Hypergamy is specific to that woman. There are many complex variables that affect what contributes to a woman's self-perception of her sexual market valuation.

For a general instance, a hot, 22 year old coed will generally be more predisposed to the Alpha Fucks side of her hypergamous impulses because she has a better capacity to capitalize on it than a 44 year old divorced mother of two. Many guys think that Hypergamy requires this endless attending to, but with the exception of outlier women, women will regulate their Hypergamy based on their self-perceived capacity to optimize it.

Simply because a woman's natural state is Hypergamy doesn't mean she is able to optimize it. She may lack opportunity (i.e. no Alpha men in the right place or at the right time), she may lack the physical appeal, she may have internalized beliefs that cause her to be more self-conscious, she may have self-esteem issues (over and under inflated), or she may simply be acculturated in a society that enforces limits upon her capacity to optimize Hypergamy. All of these limiting conditions contend with her innate hypergamous impulse.

This is the primary struggle women face; managing these limiting conditions while contending with a hard-coded Hypergamy, all before facing the inevitable, progression towards her lessened capacity to outperform her sexual competitors. Cash in too early and face the nagging doubt she could've consolidated with a more optimal man's commitment. Cash in too late and live with the consequences of settling for a suboptimal man her looks, personal conditions and societal influences allowed her to consolidate on (Alpha Widows). All of this occurs within the framework of the personal limitations (or benefits) women individually have a capacity for.

Hypergamy Unbound

One common misunderstanding most men have about Hypergamy is that it requires constant attention to mitigate. Most 'Men Going Their Own Way' (MGTOWs) follow this logic to some degree, thinking that the effort necessary to contain women's Hypergamy means this endless mind-reading or jumping through behavioral hoops in order to maintain some balance and harmony in any relationship with a woman. They believe the pay off simply isn't worth the effort, and by their individual case they may be correct, however what they don't account for is the natural balance that already exists between the genders.

Hypergamy is far easier to contain the less a woman is able to capitalize on it.

Imposing limitations on women's Hypergamy is really a matter of application. Why is our reflexive response to label possessive men as *'insecure'*? Because underneath an overt exercising of control we believe a man lacks the capacity to inspire genuine desire in a woman which prompts her to self-regulate her own Hypergamy. Yet, we still consider Mate Guarding behaviors (both conscious and subconscious) to be wise in a measured application. So there you have the line in controlling Hypergamy – like virtually anything else in Game, apply it overtly and you appear 'insecure', apply it covertly and you appear confident and in control.

To really grasp this you have to also take into account the Alpha/Beta response dynamic. Women's inborn Hypergamy will predispose women with even the most secure attachment to their mate to shit-test him.

When men become aware of this their rational minds see it as insecurity and a nuisance that they will constantly have to deal with. However, nature has engineered into our own psyches the means to deal with these tests in ways we're not really aware of. I've seen the most passive of men put their foot down after a particularly cruel shit-test and basically tell their wives or girlfriends to "shut the fuck up." It came from exasperation, but that provocation and then the response their woman got for it was exactly the requirement for passing the test.

Of course they didn't realize they were doing it, they were just pissed, lost their temper and usually apologized profusely for acting so brash after the fact. However this was exactly the response Hypergamy needed to confirm that he isn't a pushover.

Mate Guarding is another of these subliminal efforts employed to contain Hypergamy. Most men don't realize that they're manifesting mate guarding behaviors at exactly the time his woman is ovulating and more aroused by the masculine cues of an unfamiliar Alpha. Her disposition manifests in behaviors that his psyche evolved to register and reflexively trigger his own subconscious mate guarding behaviors – all in a naturalized effort to contain her innate Hypergamy. For men, nature is already aware of Hypergamy and has contingencies to limit it.

Ovulatory shift in mate preferences, and the evident behavioral shifts that result from them, prompted an evolved sensitivity to them in men. In turn, this peripheral awareness produced contingency behaviors (mate guarding) to ensure a man wasn't wasting his parental investment efforts with a child that wasn't his own.

An evolved Mate Guarding sensitivity and contingent strategy was an insurance against the cuckoldry risks inherent in women's Hypergamous sexual strategy.

I would argue that a contingent Mate Guarding strategy evolved not as a direct response to Alpha (or even Beta) competition stresses, but rather due to women's innate Hypergamy, their sexual pluralism and the potential for parental investment deception when women were left with their Hypergamy unchecked.

If a woman's predominant perception of you is Alpha, if her mental point of origin is one in which she recognizes her own SMV as being subordinate to your own, she wont be asking your "permission" to go to Las Vegas with her girlfriends for a weekend because her desire for a man she perceives as Alpha (hopefully you) will be stronger than her peers' influence on her during her ovulation week.

In theory, no woman who sees you as her perceived Alpha and Hypergamous best interest will want to 'cheat' on you – so the idea doesn't occur to her. I realize this sounds simplistic until you consider the readiness with which most men will similarly isolate themselves socially, putting off friends and family in preference to spending his time with what he believes is a high-value woman.

Another aspect of limiting Hypergamy is the inter-sexual competition women subject each other to. Hypergamy is essentially a race to the top. The higher value resources (high SMV men) drive down the cost (effort) for the lower value ones. The highest value men cascade in value by the frequency of lower value men, but it's important to remember that Hypergamy doesn't seek its own level, it always defaults to a better optimization. For a woman, the biological jackpot is to secure a commitment of genetics and resources from a mate who registers higher than herself in SMV valuation.

The very nature of Hypergamy has a culling effect for women. As if the pressures to optimize Hypergamy weren't urgent enough in the light of her personal conditions and the impending expiration of her sexual competitiveness, add to this an unforgiving intersexual competition that mitigates Hypergamy.

Thwarting Nature

If a guy swings drastically toward the Beta-chump side of the bell curve, this may well trigger a new self-perception for a woman and reinvigorate her hypergamous impulse. Likewise our current social media experience is contributing to new generations of women who lack any realistic self-image with regard to SMV and thus a false perception of their capacity to optimize their Hypergamy.

Women's overinflated sense of SMV and all the contributing factors to it is a manosphere meme now. All of these factors and more upset the balance of the Feminine Imperative with the masculine and now demand new social and psychological adaptations (i.e. formalized Game).

Many a manosphere commenter will tell you how unbound women's hypergamous nature has become since the rise of feminism and the multi-generational push to feminize every aspect of western culture. While it's true that Hypergamy "doesn't care", and many a man suffers the unprepared consequences of outdated expectations of relational equity, I don't believe the cultural shift towards the primacy of the Feminine Imperative is the doom of modern society.

To be sure, the sexual revolution and feminine-controlled ubiquitous hormonal birth control has radically shifted social primacy to the Feminine Imperative, but what this means is a readjustment of the masculine imperative is now necessary.

With the rise of the internet and the meta-Game that is the manosphere I think we're seeing this adjustment in its beginnings. In our past, society and nature evolved ways to contain Hypergamy in ways we're only peripherally aware of today, but they were serviceable contingencies that kept Hypergamy in check.

That balance will return eventually, either by men opting out of the traditional measures or women coming to a generational realization of the predicament unbridled Hypergamy and the consequences of the falsehoods fem-centrism has brought to their mothers and grandmothers.

PREVENTIVE MEDICINE

PART I

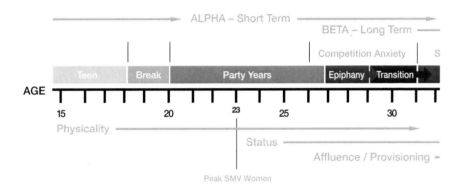

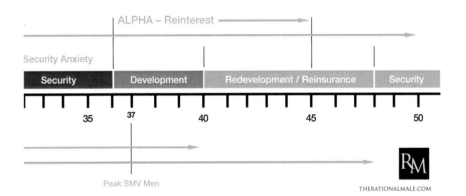

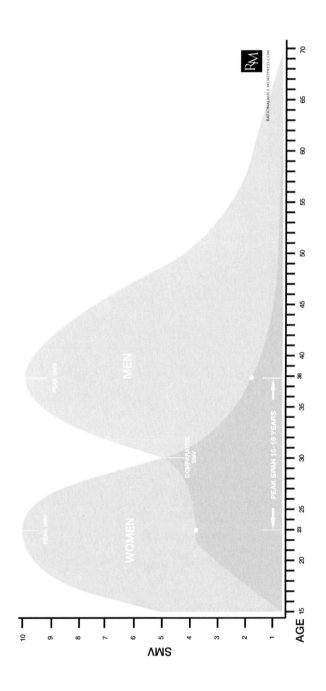

THE FORMATIVE YEARS

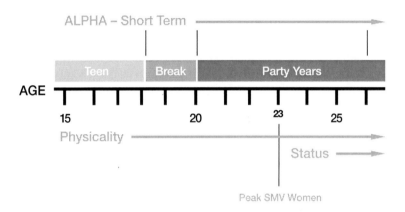

If what we refer to as Red Pill awareness has a lasting effect of any future significance, my hope is that this awareness becomes preventive medicine for young men's feminine conditioning of today.

This Red Pill awareness for men is the single greatest threat to the Feminine Imperative and feminine social primacy. I've covered aspects of this prevention in many posts on The Rational Male blog, but most were more of an after-the-fact perspective from more mature men's experiences, and how they wish they'd have known earlier in life about the Red Pill, Game and the intergender dynamics I've written about over the past 12 years of my writing.

When I originally wrote the post *Navigating the SMP* (sexual marketplace) on the blog and introduced the comparative sexual market value (SMV) chart I had no idea how influential, as well as relatively accurate, it would be in the manosphere and beyond that arena. My hope then was to educate, in a tongue-in-cheek way, a younger generation of Red Pill men about the basic schedule of how men and women's sexual market value waxes and wanes during the various phases of each sex's lifetime. This post – and more than few subsequent ones – was prompted by the desire to have an outline of what young men could generally anticipate in a contemporary, and westernized, gender landscape.

Critics of that SMV outline simplistically dismiss it as just an effort in the wishful thinking of older men convincing themselves they possess a higher sexual market value than they really warrant. However, the salient message of that graph is an uncomfortable exposing of the strategies women use in optimizing Hypergamy over the course of their lifetimes. When considered chronologically, many identifiable patterns become apparent both in women's motivations and behaviors at or around distinct phases of a woman's life.

While regarding her capacity to fulfill them at any particular phase of maturity (attractiveness), men can get a better overall idea of what is motivating a particular woman during that period of her life and adjust their Game and/or expectations accordingly to a Man's best advantage relative to that phase.

A manosphere staple, *Roissy*, wrote a fantastic piece about the difficulty of Gaming women by age brackets back in 2010, and I'll refer readers with a mind for Game to cross reference that article after reading what I propose in this section (see the appendix). With a better understanding of these phases, and the SMV fluctuations of these phases, a Man can more easily adjust his Game, maintain Frame, apply Amused Mastery, as well as a host of other Red Pill / Game practices covertly and confidently with a reasonable expectation of outcome – or at the very least, a better understanding of the personal pitfalls and traps that may await him.

One common misunderstanding most men have with regard to the way Hypergamy effects women is how the rationalizations of her past and present sexual behaviors affect a man considering marrying (or divorcing) her. What men most commonly lack, or willfully ignore, is that a woman was subject to conditions at particular periods in her life which motivated her to those behaviors – the results of which affect her present and future conditions.

I'm not sure it's realistic to expect an inexperienced man in this situation to see any of her sexual hangups or self-consciousness with him as the red flags that we can, as objective observers, and being dissociated with his condition. However, there is a certain awareness that comes with Red Pill awareness that helps us better understand what those flags are.

The armchair counseling most men offer each other usually presumes that a man should have known a woman looks for her Beta provider at the time he *happened* to 'choose' to marry her. It *happened* because at that woman's phase of life, when her sexual market value to the Jerks and Bad Boys she had an affinity for was waning, women commonly seek to consolidate long term security with the stability a Beta man provides.

But can we really expect this foresight from a guy who in all likelihood based his decisions to marry her on false romanticized premises and a thoroughly Blue Pill hope that she'd 'come around' to being more sexual (or as sexual as the more Alpha men she'd been with prior) with him later in marriage? Can we really expect him to know what her motivations were in her past for her long term security when he'd never had the benefit of ever having those motivations spelled out for him by Red Pill awareness?

It's with this in mind that I'm presenting this outline here.

What I've constructed is a loose and generalized chronology of how women effect their Hypergamy over the course of a typical woman's life between the ages of 15 and 50.

While I'm fully prepared for the same outcries of over-generalizing and the "not all women are like that" (NAWALT) rationales that the infamous SMV graph inspired, understand this; before any woman or feminine-aligned man comes up with those predictable objections, this is an *outline*. Variables like culture, ethnicity, moralism, socio-economic status and outlying circumstance are all factors to consider when evaluating the motivations and behaviors of any woman. This time line however is intended as a road map to follow to get a better understanding of what motivates women at particular phases of their lives and hopefully help men to better prepare themselves for the strategies women will use to optimize Hypergamy during those phases.

The Teen Phase

I intentionally began the original relative SMV graph at age 15 since this is about the post-pubescent age during which girls come into their maturation and teenage boys begin to take a real sexual awareness of them.

As you'll see on the overall time line, girls prioritize their attraction based on archetypal Alpha characteristics with regards to teenage attraction cues. This is largely based on physical attributes and the physical prowess of teenage boys.

These physical arousal cues girls find primarily attractive in adolescent boys (later men) will continue for the better part of a woman's life, but during a girl's formative years her foremost attraction is for the '*hawt guy*' with a good body, the correct eye color, facial symmetry and the right haircut.

Between the ages of 15 and 25 young women associate and prioritize their sexual selectivity according to men's physical features. Even a relatively introverted guy with a Beta mindset and/or a brooding 'creative' personality can still be perceived as Alpha if his physical presence aligns with a girl's physical attraction profile.

The main reasoning for this is fairly obvious in that physical cues (though also influenced externally) are primarily innate. In other words, a teenage girl simply doesn't have the life experience or a sense of provisioning necessity for much else to be an attraction consideration for her. Her mate prioritization cues on visceral arousal. Thus, this physical interest from adolescence through young adulthood is the top priority for both short term arousal and, perceptually, long-term attraction.

These physical attraction / arousal cues are intrinsic. Extrinsic attraction cues such as status and social proof do factor in progressively as girls mature, but the priority is the physical. Other extrinsic factors (status, Alpha confidence, Game, etc.), while peripherally beneficial, are prioritized lower due to the simple fact that a young girl lacks any real experience of a guy with Game, social savvy or a *real* need for personal or emotional provisioning.

Note that all of this is predicated on a variety of external existing resources. There is a whole lot of support for young women that is not visible to them, and that support is a product of a tremendous excess of resources at the society-wide level as well as the family level.

Long term provisioning potential during this phase is rarely even an afterthought for a young woman. From adolescence forward a woman's dualistic sexual strategy primarily revolves around short term breeding opportunity – the 'Alpha Fucks' side of Hypergamy. This can be attributed to a girl / young woman's provisioning needs being relatively accommodated for by family, the state in some effect, or even her own self-provisioning, as well as the breeding urgency that comes with puberty, hormones and youth culture.

I'll add the caveat here that a woman's prioritization of the physical is inversely proportional to the degree to which her provisioning needs are being met beyond seeking a mate or mating opportunities. In other words, if things aren't secure at home (Daddy Issues) an adolescent girl physically and mentally prepares herself for a long term mate earlier than when a solid, positive-masculine father is present in her life and in the home.

This can be a precarious situation for a teenage girl since her maturity and understanding of what would make a man a good long-term prospect are limited by what she lacks in a positive-masculine role, and combined with an attraction priority that's based on the physical attributes of a teenage boy.

The short version for teenage Game (when you're in high school) is that looks, physique and physical prowess are a girl's attraction priority. This priority will build a foundation for her attraction cues later as she matures, but the primary importance during this phase is looks and performance.

The Break Phase

I've added this phase to the end of the late teen years because this 'breaking' event has become an increasingly too common, and potentially damaging, occurrence amongst young men I've counseled.

Generally the Break Phase comes at or about the time of a young woman's senior year (or shortly thereafter) of high school when she's forced into a conflict between continuing a monogamous relationship she began in her teenage years, and severing it as college or a simple want for sexual independence looms closer as she approaches young adulthood, graduation and possibly moving away from her home for an indefinite period of time.

This is a major frustration for Beta minded young men predisposed to a feminized conditioning that convinces them they'll be rewarded for loyalty, support and building relational equity with a girl. I'm highlighting this phase because often enough it's at this beginning point young men are most prepared to compromise their life's ambitions to play the idealistic supportive role their feminine conditioning predisposes them for. The danger being that long-term life decisions made in order to maintain a relationship he believes his sacrifices will be rewarded for will be an equitable sacrifice of personal goals or developing passions and personal potential.

Here is the warning for any late teen / early adult man: This is generally the point at which you'll have to make some real personal assessments of yourself if you're involved with a steady girlfriend. This will likely be the first test of your Red Pill awareness conflicting with your feminine-primary conditioning. Most Blue Pill guys entertain the hope of the 'invisible friend', and a long distance relationship for the first time at this juncture. That or they alter their educational priorities and ambitions to accommodate maintaining their relationship.

Statistically, the girlfriend you expected to build a Disney-story life with will break up with you as her options expand and yours constrict (due to prioritizing her goals above your own). If this is your situation the decisions you make at this stage are up to you, but understand (barring personal convictions) this event will come as a woman's sexual market value begins it's rapid ascent and along with it personal and sexual opportunities she's been scarcely aware of until now.

The Party Years

The five year span between 20 and 25 are what I euphemistically call a woman's 'Party Years'. It's at this stage women generally experience their peak SMV (22-23 years old), and as I stated in the *Navigating the SMP* post, at no other point in a woman's life will so many socio-sexual options be available to her.

A lot of manosphere moralists believe that women ought to marry and get pregnant during the party years since this is the point of peak fertility as well as physical beauty, and in the not so distant, pre-sexual revolution past this certainly made sense. However, under the social conditions of the last 60 years, women's priorities have changed.

The available opportunities – social, sexual, educational and career-wise – that a woman experiences during these years are afforded to her in relation to her SMV. At no point will you find a woman more cocky and self-assured of her predominance in society according to the options she enjoys relative to her attractiveness. Her personal image will be one based on merit, and while it's certainly possible she is talented or intelligent, her opportunities are predicated on her attractiveness and the leverage it has on other's (men and women's) decision making.

The physical arousal priorities she had in high school remain a top attraction priority, however, as she matures into the new experiences her SMV peak affords her, status, and later affluence (wealth or potential provisioning) start getting added to the attraction mix. As women learn the utility of their relative SMV, and begin to understand a future need for long term provisioning (on some level of consciousness) they come into a better understanding of the transactional nature of their sexual agency.

It's during the party years that women begin to prefer 'dating' men older than themselves. At this phase this is generally between a 4-6 year difference, however, *Roissy* postulated that even more mature men still have potential depending upon their own SMV:

> *It may be hard to believe, but it is often easier to bed a very young woman than an older woman, if you are an older man. This is because 20-40% of women are specifically attracted to older men. It is hard-wired in them, and this hard-wiring can be reinforced by poor family upbringing resulting from divorce of parents or absentee fathers. Single moms are the greatest source of future generations of slutty daughters the world has ever known.*

During the party years, Hypergamy is still firmly rooted in physical attraction and short term mating cues, however, it's during this time women begin to develop an appreciation for the personality cues of confidence and (Alpha) character as it relates to her long term investment.

Later in the party years a woman's Hypergamy leads her to look for the Alpha bad boy who might also be molded (tamed) into her long term ideal – this is the Tarzan Effect; the want for an idealized optimal balance of hypergamic interests in the *same* Alpha male. The idea is one that an Alpha Man might be tamed, in some cases coerced via pregnancy, into assuming the providership role (Beta Bucks) the other half of her sexual strategy demands.

One point of attraction older men (who capitalize on their SMV potential) have is that their capacity to provide for more than themselves, and still maintain an above average physique, tends to be a form of preselection for this burgeoning awareness of a need for hypergamic balance as women mature past the latter part of their party years.

Just to be clear, as a woman becomes more cognizant of her decreasing capacity to sexually compete with the attractiveness of younger women, her attraction for more than just the physical aspects of men begins to assume a higher priority. Those aspects (status, confidence, affluence, realized ambitions, worldly maturity, etc.) are typically found in men old enough to have had the experience to acquire them.

Social Conventions

Many of the predominant social conventions that persist through the Teen, Pre-Adult and early Party Years phases find their roots in women's childhoods. These conventions may be more or less pronounced for a teenage girl depending on her parents' involvement in her upbringing, but popular culture and a feminine-primary social order already have a pre-established series of conventions she's expected to invest herself in.

For the most part these conventions key upon an implied superiority of her gender while ridiculing any valuable aspect of masculinity beyond a Beta boy's oafish usefulness to her. These conventions are generally learned in an ambient environment that boys are encouraged to reinforce and affirm for her, but increasingly these social conventions are becoming overt and accepted.

By a girl's 'tween' years she's seen enough Disney feminine-empowerment features that the expectations and concerns of girls becomes one less about meriting the near-valueless attentions of mediocre boys and more about the girls who will eventually become her intrasexual rivals.

Little girls fight in an entirely different realm than do boys. Where boys fight in a the physical realm, girls fight in the psychological. That's not to exclude girls from actually coming to blows, but far more common is the occurrence of psychological combat, and in no realm is this more effective than the denial of reinforcing attention within a female social collective.

Little girls have a predictable tendency to form small, girl-only collectives or 'peer clutches' from the time they are introduced into kindergarten. This social collective progressively becomes a rewarding and reinforcing social unit, locking out those not included, and nurturing those who are included.

This dynamic can last through high school (i.e. cliques, etc.), into college and into mature adulthood, but the commonality within all variations of this clutch is the qualifying influence of the affirming power of attention. Should one member offend another, it's the hierarchy of an individual member's ability to maintain the most attention that generally determines the victor in the dispute.

The worst consequence of such a dispute being ostracization from the group, thus the absolute denial of this reaffirming attention-as-reinforcement. This attention can be from any source; within the group, outside the group, but opposite sex attention becomes the most valuable after puberty. Attention-attraction capacity denotes social rank within the peer clutch. The more attractive the girl, the more popular she becomes and the more influence she wields. This isn't to say that any particular girl cognizantly realizes this.

However, when ostracized from the collective, this capacity for consistently attracting attention in a high degree makes her despised. The attention can still be beneficial for affirmation (i.e. realized jealousy), it's just the intent that has changed.

Thus, women use attention not only for their own affirmation, individually and collectively, but also to do combat with each other. Far more damaging than physical fighting is the long term psychological impact of denying this reinforcing satisfaction of attention, or better still, delegitimizing or disqualifying a girl / woman's capacity to attract this attention. Combine this with a woman's natural, and innately higher agency to communicate both verbally and non-verbally (i.e. covert communications) and you can see the potential this has in damaging a rival. This might explain a woman's natural propensity to gossip.

When a woman attacks the respectability and character of another ("she's such a slut"), in essence, she is assaulting the woman's agency for garnering attention by delegitimizing it.

Attention is the coin of the realm in girl-world, and this is an aspect of the feminine psyche that men would be wise to remember during all stages of women's maturity. Attention is valuable to both the twelve year old girl learning how to apply her first makeup and the eighty year old matron applying it for so long she can't remember not doing it.

Outliers

There are of course going to be incidents of women who, for some condition or circumstance opt out of their party years. Either their socioeconomic situation prevents it, or an early, unplanned pregnancy, or for religious convictions, but whatever the reason they move past this phase without a sense of having capitalized on it.

In some respects this may seem to be a better choice than riding the proverbial 'cock carousel' into her Epiphany and Transitory phase (discussed in the next chapter), but it's important to remember that these circumstances don't disqualify a woman from the maturation process I've described here, they simply manifest relative behaviors in alternative ways.

In some cases it may be the source of resentment at a man for having 'held her back' from all of the experiences her girlfriends went through (through which she vicariously lived), or it may be her coming into a better understanding of how other men (perceptually) meet her hypergamic balance better than the one she settled for earlier than she had the maturity to understand. As we'll explore in the next chapter, this resentment can be a later source of marital dissatisfaction (and divorce) for women approaching the Epiphany and Transitory phases.

The Break Phase is also an important concept to grasp here. While it commonly first occurs around the time of high school graduation, a Break Phase isn't limited to that period. The Break can come later, when a woman is finishing up college or just prior to, or starting a job or grad school. Commonly a later Break Phase generally happens during women's peak SMV or around the ages of 22 to 25.

There could also be more than one Break Phase – one at around 18, and another at around 22 or 23 depending on the context and circumstances of a young woman's life.

Later Breaks seem to occur with women at the time of major life events – high school graduation, college graduation, moving to a new locale, making a career move. In general, the events and the conditions leading up to them is what a man needs to be most aware of in anticipating a Break Phase crisis with a woman.

The reason a woman has a Break is that her circumstances are changing; which affects her emotions. She's changing her surroundings and then there's how she feels about that change, and how she considers a man's involvement in that change.

The other thing to keep in mind around Breaks is that the crisis forces her to make a decision about whether the change is more important than the man she is with when the Break happens. In a feminine-primary social order most of the time she decides that the change is more important. This is likely because, women are acculturated in a social order that reinforces women's aspirations and 'empowerment', and encourages her to postpone intimate and family relations until she attains some nebulous goal state. At that time she will always be able to find another man (or so she's told).

Needless to say this section is designed to help young men make better life choices by making them aware of what they can expect in their adolescence and young adulthood. Hold this outline in your head and plan accordingly, but also I think it should help a guy get a better perspective of the events he'll likely find himself in and understand the influences he's subject to by the women he involves and associates himself with.

If you're a young man reading this section, my best advice is to consider that the decisions and circumstances you're confronted with today will drastically change in less than a decade. Understand that making life-changing emotional or idealistically motivated decisions now will affect the direction of your life.

That might sound like something your old man or a school counselor will tell you in your senior year – I know because you couldn't tell me shit when I was in my senior year – but what they wont tell you (because they're conditioned to ignore it) is that the "do the right thing" idealism you think will be reciprocally appreciated by a girl or a young woman is part of a feminine-primary conditioning you've been raised in.

You are the hardest reader to reach from a Red Pill perspective because young men are taught to believe that the more you suffer, the more you support, the more you lift up a girlfriend to help her realize her dreams at the cost of your own, the more it shows you really care.

A final thought to remember – with the exception of the most necessitous and the most ethically convicted, most women in the developed world are literally incapable of committing to anything between 18-20 and not just because they've got some naive ideas in their head, but because they literally just walked into the candy store, and they're not about to leave with the first flavor they try.

It's important to remember this now, because it will be a double standard women will hold for men later in life. "Men are commitment-phobic" is a popular social convention trope women like to repeat when they reach an age where their own SMV is in decline (The Epiphany Phase) and they want to cash out of the sexual marketplace with a man they can consolidate a long term provisioning with.

As that man enters his SMV ascendancy and he enters the "candy store" the commitment imperative she enjoyed around 19 changes for him at 33. This is the parallel men will experience in respect to commitment; he is responsible to commitment with a woman, while she is responsible in exploring all her options.

PREVENTIVE MEDICINE

PART II

THE EPIPHANY PHASE

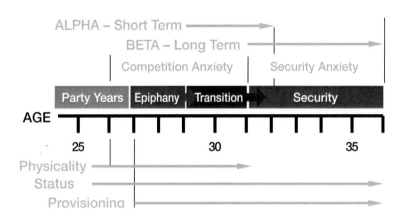

The Late Party Years

Although not a subsection itself, the latter third of a woman's Party Years deserves some mention in that the end of this phase is often a prelude for the rationales women develop leading into what I call the Epiphany Phase. Certain third party SMV studies (online dating site informatics for instance) will place a woman's peak SMV as late as 25-26 years old. While this is generous for women's sensibilities, I'd argue that this is far too late in a woman's life progression when you consider that in earlier eras, men and women achieved social adulthood at much earlier ages.

More commonly in our times most women express a desire to settle down, be married and start a family at or around the age of 27 to 29, and most first marriages do in fact happen at an average age of 28 (U.S. Census data corroborates this for 2013).

The popularized, ideal of a woman capitalizing on her prime earning years – often excused as fulfilling her professional potential – is a primary contributor to this marriage postponement phenomenon, but it's important to point out to men dating women in this phase that the last two years of the Party phase will be the stage at which a woman will begin to feel a more pressing urgency for long-term commitment.

It's during this phase that women, with the foresight to see it, will make their best attempts to consolidate on marriage with the man who best personifies, or has the potential to personify, both Alpha sexual-genetics combined with the providership and parental investment that an optimized Hypergamy *seeks* to balance in the same man. At no other time will a woman feel more urgency in capitalizing on her still prime attractiveness and sexual agency with a man she believes will fulfill the dual dictates of her sexual strategy.

"Where is this going?"

This is the most common phase in which a man will be asked "where is this going?" from a woman, or is delivered an ultimatum of withdrawal of intimacy (no more sex, or threats of break up) if no marriage proposal is forthcoming in the foreseeable future.

Although women's preferred method of communication rests in the covert form, as she matures towards a condition of a lessened capacity to intra-sexually compete with her younger peers (competition anxiety) most men discover that women in this demographic, by necessity, lean more on overt communication.

The coquetry, indirectness and blasé indifference she used to enjoy and hold male attentions captive during her SMV peak years is progressively replaced with a more direct upfront communication directed toward the certainty of promised, committed, assurances of future security.

The urgency of her need to consolidate on a supportive monogamy intensifies in direct relation to the intrasexual competition stress she experiences as she ages and her sexual market value declines in comparison to that competition. This urgency makes the need for overt communication (men's direct content based communication) increasingly more imperative for her so there is less and less margin for men to misunderstand her need.

Bear in mind that security for women isn't always manifested as financial provisioning, but can assume the forms of emotional investment, parental investment, physical security and, most importantly, fulfilling a psychological need for a masculine role of stability, dominance and direction in her life.

Of primary importance is the consideration of women's drive to realize the Alpha Fucks / Beta Bucks (AFBB) optimized balance of their hypergamous interests in the same man at this stage. That's not to say this isn't always the operative for feminine Hypergamy, but it's during the late Party Years phase that a woman, on some level of consciousness, begins to realize this time is her best opportunity to use her quick-burn SMV to consolidate on what she thinks *could* be a realizable optimized Hypergamy. This isn't due to premonitions of hitting the Wall of her SMV potential per se, but it is her first self-acknowledgment of her diminishing capacity to sexually compete for attention with her competition for that optimized guy – younger women experiencing their own SMV peak years.

During this period women will often make their first earnest attempts to find ways – sometimes by coercion – to 'fix' an Alpha into satisfying the Beta Bucks side of her Hypergamy equation, or, to seriously reevaluate an already committed Beta man's potential to 'Man Up' and become more Alpha, be more ambitious and assesses (what she believes will be) his future SMV potential.

Lastly, bear in mind that women in this phase experience this urgency in direct proportion to what their looks, sexuality and command of male attention will still afford them. It's simple reasoning to figure that women who maintain their physical attractiveness and sexual agency, and are consistently rewarded for it with male attention, will prolong that state for as long as possible. Thus, some attractive women may perpetuate their Party Years until such time as that attention abruptly ends.

The Epiphany and Transitory Phase

Between the ages of 28 to about 30 (sometimes later for attractive women per-petuating their Party Years) women often enter into a more cognitive awareness of their personal conditions with regard to their declining SMV. This phase I call The Epiphany Phase; it is the point at which the subconscious awareness a woman has of her sexual market value in relation to her eventual date with the Wall can no longer be subconsciously repressed and ignored.

It is of primary importance to men to fully understand the significance this phase has for women. Again, the epiphany isn't about women hitting their SMV Wall during this phase (though it's possible) it's about a woman conscientiously coming to terms with a markedly lessened capacity to sexually compete with her SMV-peak peers for the same male attention she enjoyed during her Party Years.

The abstract exaggeration is to think a woman necessarily hits the Wall at 30, her physical attractiveness shrivels and she magically transforms into a spinster cat lady overnight. Women absolutely (with commensurate effort) can and often do retain their looks and sexual agency past this phase; some into their late 30's and 40's. However, what defines this phase is the conscious realization that their looks are no longer what they were in their prime.

Combined with this is the awareness that they can no longer sexually compete at the *same* level as young women in their own SMV peaks for the attentions of men they now hope to consolidate their Hypergamy on in long-term commitment and provisioning security.

The Epiphany phase isn't about women hitting the Wall so much as it is about an urgency to consolidate upon a man's commitment of long-term security with the competition anxiety that comes from realizing it's now *she* who must to put forth the effort to secure it rather than having it readily offered to her as it was by the men in her SMV peak years.

This is a precarious time for a woman where she makes attempts to reassess the last decade of her life. Women's psychological rationalization engine (a.k.a. the Hamster) begins a furious effort to account for, and explain her reasonings for not having successfully secured a long-term monogamous commitment from as Alpha a man as her attractiveness could merit for her. Even women married prior to this phase (early marriages) will still go through some variation of self-doubt, or self-pity in dealing with the hypergamic uncertainty of her choice ("Is he really the best I could do?").

A woman's late Party Years are often the stage during which she entertains the hope that she can 'civilize' the Alpha Bad Boys who satisfy the visceral side of her Hypergamy into assuming the providership role the other side of her Hypergamy demands, and is increasingly becoming more urgent for her.

Most Alpha Widows – women who psychologically imprint on the psycho-sexual ideal of the most Alpha man she's been involved with in her sexual past – are most commonly made during this period. However, it's during the Epiphany phase women conveniently make the rationalizations necessary for justifying this 'fixing' effort.

During the Epiphany Phase a woman's inner and outer dialog is self-excusing, virtuously self-educational and self-congratulatory.

"I used to be so different in college, but I've grown personally" or "I've learned my lesson about pursuing the 'wrong kind' of men, I'm done with Bad Boys now" and "What happened to all the Nice Men?" are the standard clichés women will tell themselves.

Women will broadcast these rationalizations, either directly or indirectly, to men with a providership potential in the hopes of signaling to them that she is now ready accept their feminine-preconditioned offers of love, loyalty and dependability – offers which had been regularly forthcoming from men in the past, but she had no use of in during her Party Years.

This phase is a functional parallel to men's feminine-imagined midlife crisis.

It's during this stage that women will make radical shifts in their prioritization of what prerequisite traits qualify as 'attractive' in a man and attempt to turn over a new leaf by changing up their behaviors to align with this new "do-it-right-girl" persona they create for themselves.

Since the physicality, sexual prowess and Alpha dominance that made up her former arousal cues in a Man aren't quite as forthcoming from men as when she was in her sexual prime, she reprioritizes them with presumed preferences for more intrinsic male attributes that stress dependability, provisioning capacity or potential for it, humor, intellect, and esoteric definitions of compatibility and intimacy. All of which fall in line with her new sense of self-convinced feminine maturity and wisdom.

For the metaphysically inclined woman (which is to say most women) this may manifest in a convenient return to religious convictions she'd disregarded or abandoned in her Party Years. For other's it may be some kind of self-enforced celibacy – a refusal to have sex under the Hypergamic auspices of her Party Years in the hopes that a well provisioning male will appreciate her for her 'new found' prudence, so unlike how she used to be and all of the other girls who rejected him over the last decade.

The self-affirming psychological schema is one where she's "finally doing the right thing" or she's determined to make a fresh start "the right way this time", when in fact she's simply making the necessity of her long-term security a virtue she hopes the "right" men will appreciate. And if they don't, then there's always the social convention of shaming them to think they're 'less-than-men' for not forgiving her of eating her cake once she's had it too.

While looks and masculine physical triggers in men are still an important arousal factor, her desire for a personal association with a man's status and affluence begin to sublimate her physical priorities for attraction as she increasingly realizes the necessity of these attributes for herself and any future offspring's long-term provisioning. It should be noted that the appeal of a man's potential for provisioning is proportional to her perceived need of that provisioning.

The Transitioning

As a woman moves into the Transitory phase (29-31) the Epiphany Phase repri- oritizing of intrinsic attraction cues also coincides with the adjusted self-percep- tion of her own sexual market value.

As a woman becomes more cognizant of her lessened ability to sexually compete for men who (she believes) would meet her best Hypergamic balance, she's forced to reassess her self-image.

There are many feminine social conventions pre-established to help her deny or buffer this reassessment. However, her hindbrain still acknowledges the competi- tion anxiety that (unless, by effort or genetics, she's a notable physical exception) she simply cannot command the kind of male attention women in their SMV-peak years do. Thus she must imagine value added aspects for herself and convince men that if they don't appreciate those newly-contrived aspects as valuable their value as a man is lessened.

Note that the reality of this assessment, or realistic expectations of it, aren't the source of this anxiety, but rather it's what she *believes* them to be.

An exceptionally attractive 30 year old woman may in fact still be able to sex- ually select men above what most women her age can expect, however it's what she *believes* about herself, her internalized expectations for her age and what the Party Years experience has or hasn't taught her in this respect that contributes to this anxiety. As you may guess this self-assessment is also subject to the influences of social media and social conventions that pander to insulating her from the worst damage to her ego of this Epiphany and the Transition period's anxiety.

There's a manosphere idiom that states the only women who complain about men needing to Man Up or how men have somehow juvenilely shirked the mas- culine responsibilities society expects of them are always 30 years of age or older. Younger women simply have no incentive to complain about what they believe they are entitled to in a man beyond his being 'hawt'.

What I term as the Transition phase is the culmination of the Epiphany phase's influence on a woman who has thus far been unable to consolidate on monoga- my with a male who fulfills the role of provider (Beta provider most often) that her Hypergamy now holds in a much higher priority order. When women in this phase complain of men's "adequacy issues" what they're really bemoaning is their chronic inability to find (or merit) a man who can optimally balance the dual influences of her Hypergamy – Alpha Fucks and Beta Bucks.

The urgency for this consolidation is then compounded by the misconceptions most women hold about the Myth of their Biological clock, but in biological terms she's well past the years of her prime fertility window and conceiving and carrying a child to term becomes progressively more difficult for women with each passing year.

I think it's important to consider other outcomes of personal decisions women often do make during these periods. As I mentioned in Part I, it's not uncommon for some women to consolidate on monogamy (LTR or marriage) well before either of these phase take place. While the experiences may differ, the underlying influences that prompt these phases remain more or less the same. I'll elaborate more on this in Part III as it primarily relates to the later phases of women's maturation process.

Social Conventions

In the Transition phase, the competition anxiety that prompted the Epiphany Phase is exchanged for an anxiety that results from confronting the possibility a woman may *never* consolidate on a long-term security. However, as always, feminine social conventions are already in place to absolve her of any real personal accountability for this insight.

Thus, begins the 'Men are threatened by powerful women', 'Men have fragile egos', 'Men are shallow and only want young girls they can manipulate instead of vibrant women who are their intellectual equals' and various other canards intended to simultaneously shame men into compliance with their hypergamous imperative. These ready conventions are established to relieve women of any personal accountability for the anxiety the Transition phase forces them to experience.

For Red Pill, Game-aware Men, the Epiphany phase is a supremely important stage in women's maturation to consider.

A woman in the Epiphany Phase is looking for a "fresh start" for a much more visceral reason than some newly inspired sense of self. This motivation prompts all kinds of behavioral and social conventions to facilitate a man's commitment to forgiving her past indiscretions. As I mentioned, it's women in this phase of life (or the mothers of women in this phase) who most vocally complain about men's lack of interest in committing to them.

Women in their peak SMV years don't complain about a dearth of marriageable men– "Man Up" is the anthem of women in the Epiphany Phase.

Operative social conventions abound for women in their late Party Years, through their Epiphany and Transitioning Phases, and not until their mid-thirties does the usefulness of these phases' conventions really shift to more useful ones.

Most of these center on two primary aspects of a woman's maturity. The first being the necessity of absolving a woman of the consequences of following the dictates her hypergamous sexual strategy incurred for her. The Party Years are defined by a woman prioritizing the Alpha Fucks side of Hypergamy. Post-Party Years social conventions euphemistically refer to this as a woman finding herself or "exploring her options", but this period is defined by the "bad decisions" women characteristically make with men who "weren't really good for them".

That isn't to say all women make these mistakes, but even the most reserved of women still prioritize Alpha excitement above Beta comfort and familiarity.

"I was looking for love in all the wrong places."

"I always wanted marriage. I always wanted to find a great guy to settle down and have kids with. It just never happened for me."

"I made a lot of mistakes." (I made a lot of decisions that seemed like a good idea in the moment but when aggregated make me look kind of bad to you now.)

"I didn't intend to get to 30 without being married. It just kind of happened."

The common thread running through all this is the woman's having sex with various attractiveness-prioritized men with options in the hopes that one of them would offer her commitment on her terms. When she fails in her attempt to get one of these top men to commit, she has to find a way to rationalize it so as to put the best face on it she can. The simplest way of ego preservation is to say "well, I always wanted to get married all along; it just never worked out for whatever reason". And this is why men hear these rationalizations and explanations for the "crazy pasts they're over now", the Alpha men they can't seem to get over (Alpha Widows) and the first night lays they had.

The second necessity for operative social conventions dovetails with the first in that they aid in consolidating on Beta provisioning and parental investment by ensuring those men remain compliant to what their own feminine conditioning has prepared them for.

Women's long term security and provisioning depends on a man never fully coming into an awareness of his true SMV until after a woman can consolidate on his commitment to her. Scarier still is the thought that a man might come to that awareness after his potential has been compromised and limited by the decisions he was led to believe were his responsibilities to the feminine imperative and can never fully realize because of those decisions.

Social convention that key on presumed social responsibility bombard men from all sides during this phase of women's maturity – even perpetuated by men themselves.

"Men should date women their own age."

"Men are 'shallow' for ignoring single mothers as viable long term mates."

"Men have 'fragile egos' needing constant affirmation in an infantile respect."

"Men feel threatened by 'successful' women."

These are a few examples but the prevalent social conventions of this phase all key on appeals to (Beta) men's presumed social responsibility, shame and emphasizing a man's 'duty' to abandoning or compromising his own sexual strategy's best interests.

The Cardinal Rule of Sexual Strategies
For one gender's sexual strategy to succeed the other
gender must compromise or abandon their own.

In no other phase of maturity is it more vital for a man to understand what this rule means in terms of having his future life's plans dictated to him by the Feminine Imperative. Every social convention employed at this key period has the latent purpose of convincing a man that his sexual strategy should be congruent with a woman's sexual strategy (Hypergamy). Those conventions' purpose is to convince him it is his uniquely male duty to fulfill and forgive the trappings of a woman's drive for optimal Hypergamy and thus ensure the success of her sexual strategy.

The imperative of those conventions is to convince him of such before he comes to a full realization of his peak sexual market value, and thus putting a man into the prime sexual selector position. Men in such an awareness of their own SMV become a threat to women's control of their own Hypergamy.

One of the greatest misdirections of gender understanding over the past 60 years has been the idea that both men and women *should* share the same sexual strategy. A naive equalitarian ideology dictates the need for both genders to have equally similar, cooperative gender life goals, and equally similar methods to realize them. But as with most feminine-primary social engineering, Mother Nature and men and women's biological imperatives are always at odds with this.

Generally this assimilation of a common sexual strategy is ingrained early on in men's feminization conditioning. I use the term 'assimilation' because men are taught and conditioned to presume that the feminine sexual strategy (however most women subjectively choose to define it) is universally the *correct* strategy – and any deviation from what ultimately serves feminine Hypergamy is met with ridicule at best, accusations of misogyny and ostracization at worst.

Hypergamy essentially revolves around optimizing (and maximally protracting) women's unilateral sexual selection from Good Genes men (direct benefits) and Good Dad's men (material benefits). Alpha Fucks / Beta Bucks.

From a biological perspective men's sexual imperative is one of unlimited access to unlimited sexual availability. This isn't to discount the very strong impulse in men to seek assurances of paternity in the children they ultimately sire, however, prior to his parental investment, the male impetus is to seek unlimited access to unlimited sexuality.

When we consider a male sexual imperative in the biological respect, and the strategies men use to effect it, it becomes easier to understand the social conventions and engineering the Feminine Imperative uses to control and maximally restrict men as sexual selectors.

Outliers

There are infinite paths a woman's search for commitment could take, opening up the possibility of a second dimension to the time line wherein diversions from the "worst case" path of no-commitment are entertained for period where Beta provisioning is secured, or Alphas are found.

All sorts of things could change; the Party Years might be extremely compressed, or even non-existent. The Break Phase might actually be pushed back because a more Alpha lover limited a woman's vision of her own options. The Epiphany and Transition Phases probably exists in some form for all women, but in happily married women those phases come out looking less like panic.

For women who consolidate on monogamy prior to those phases their experiences are more like a regretful realizations of getting older, and (sometimes grudgingly) seeing the actualized value in her husband as he progresses toward his own SMV peak years.

This is yet another purpose of keeping men ignorant of women's sexual strategies until they can consolidate on monogamy. So long as he's educated and conditioned for most of his life to be an ideal, dependable Beta his sense of social responsibility to his wife should be an insurance for her long term security when he finally does come to realize his SMV potential.

One of the problems men encounter with women who are 'early consolidators' is that they risk being associated with the consequences of the regret a woman feels as she proceeds through these phases tied down by commitments to monogamy or resulting children.

These women are beset on many fronts by a social order that emphasizes (and glorifies) female empowerment. They cannot avoid the social awareness that they live in an unprecedented era when women's opportunities for self-advancement coincides with women's unilateral control of their own Hypergamy. The message is one of the world being a woman's oyster both professionally and sexually, why would any gal want to saddle herself with a less than optimal man and a less than rewarding personal/professional life?

That's a tough message to swallow, but furthermore she's forced to live vicariously through these phases with her single friends and a ceaseless media broadcasting its message and catering to her need for indignation while she lives a "less than" life of committed early monogamy only advancing yearly towards the Wall.

For men who consolidate early, and likely idealistically, with this outlier, his Blue Pill mindset is challenged as her discontent evolves towards her Epiphany Phase. Her single girlfriends are experiencing a very different life and she shares that from a distance her commitment wont allow her to get any closer to.

When a woman spends the better part of her twenties sharing the second-hand indignation and sexual adventures of her peers while living in the constraints of monogamous commitment, her Epiphany Phase becomes one of a last chance at a second chance. Divorce fantasy stories and movies are directed primarily at this outlier and grow in popularity. The man she married in her youth is at last revealed as the Beta schlub he is (despite all past dedication and performance) and she consoles herself with the possibilities of enjoying the kinds of Alpha lovers her girlfriends regaled her with in their experiences for the past ten or so years.

This type of Epiphany and Transitioning Phase is still rooted in a woman's realization that she wont be able to sexually compete with younger versions of herself, but that realization stems from her awareness that this phase is her last chance for a "good life". Courtesy of the experiences of her girlfriends and what she takes for her own seasoned maturity, she now sees her dedicated Beta as "just a guy" and a guy who'll never get it.

She loves him, but she's not *in* love with him. His reality doesn't compare to the fantasy she resents him for preventing her from experiencing. She missed out, and the epiphany becomes one of risking it all for one last chance at it.

A Note on Ultimatums

One area I felt I should mention here is that during this stage of a woman's maturity, men will commonly be delivered ultimatums – "Marry me or we're through" or "You need to fix this about yourself if we're going to be together."

Ultimatums are declarations of powerlessness because you are resorting to a direct threat to get someone to do what you want them to, and in doing so you *overtly* confess your weak position. If a woman were in a genuine position of control it wouldn't be necessary to resort to an ultimatum; she'd simply use that control (as she likely did in her Party Years). There are many ways to effect a change in another person, but ultimatums will never prompt a *genuine* change. If they change behavior it's prompted by the threat, not unprompted, organic desire.

This is important to remember because a relationship based on a man acquiescing to a woman's ultimatum fundamentally corrupts the Frame and future of that marriage / relationship. Agreeing to an ultimatum is both negotiated desire and a permanent impression of your Beta status to a woman.

One of the primary tenets of my Game philosophy is that true desire cannot be negotiated. A natural, unsolicited desire state, unmitigated by obligation or concerns for resources exchange, is the ideal basis for any intergender relationship. Any factors that introduce elements that hinder this genuine desire – exchange, negotiations, obligations, reciprocity, etc. – weaken this desire and weaken the relationship. Delivering an ultimatum is the most direct, overt way to introduce exactly these elements into a relationship.

You cannot effect a genuine change of desire with an ultimatum as your relationship will be founded on that threat. This is the real power issue; that a woman would want a man to conform to her desire so badly that she'd use a threat to effect it despite the foreknowledge that it can never be a genuine conformation.

Hypergamy only believes the dominance of a man that a woman finds in him, never the dominance a woman needs to create in him.

Betas at the Epiphany – Saving the Best

"I Would Never Have dated You When I Was 25"

I had a friend relate this conversation to me. This is what his girlfriend blurted out to him right before he'd told her he would never marry her.

She proceeded to explain how "back in the day" she was attracted to bodybuilder types and how she found them disgusting now. The truth was depressing for him. He managed to maintain Frame pretty well when she said this, but mainly because he'd only just remembered that she said it about an hour before.

"The truth is, I wanted to weep. I wanted to weep not just because I'm getting the leftovers. But also because her female mind will make sure she never understands.

And also because I'm going to have to leave this girl soon if she expects me to invest more into her than I deem her worthy. And I wanted to weep because I honestly feel like she might be lost without me due to her mental illnesses and lack of self control. And I wanted to weep because I know she will fuck men left and right after we break up. I wanted to weep because I fell in love with her no matter how many times I told myself not to. What kind of fucked up game is this?"

His situation is the most common frustration men in this demographic experience with women on the other side of their Epiphany and Transition phases – the harsh realization that what he was convinced would be his wife's sexual best would be his in a committed marriage.

To really understand the Security Phase men need to grasp the long term effects of women's dualistic strategy on the Beta man's mindset as a result of his feminine-centric conditioning.

When a woman approaches and enters into her Epiphany Phase, she has a limbic understanding that her genetic chips need to be cashed in with a man who has 'proper' long term provisioning potential. For the greater part, those men are expected by women to have some Blue Pill conditioning that will make them more compliant with what's now becoming an unignorable form of open Hypergamy.

Prior to technologies that could evidentially prove women's sexual exploits, the more visceral aspects of a woman's sexuality, and the inconvenient hind-brain/hormonal prompts that motivate them, could be kept secret well enough to deceive men with provisioning potential to commit to long term security. As the technology to record this becomes more ubiquitous, more permanent and fluid in its use, (and as men become more interconnected by it) rationalizing those evident past 'indiscretions' becomes more of an imperative for women.

Men saturated and conditioned over the better half of their lifetime by the feminine imperative to be the convenient cuckolds to women's Hypergamy – men like my friend in this confession – have an ego-invested interest in presuming the woman they pair with will be "giving him the best of herself" once his ship comes in and all of his patience and equalist beliefs finally pay off.

Only, men like this discover too late – usually well after they realize their commitment has hamstrung their SMV peak potential – that not only have they been a retroactive cuckold (sometimes moralistically proud to be so), but they've been socially conditioned to be one, by their mothers, their emasculated fathers, their sisters, female friends, teachers and the whole of the Feminine Imperative's effort for most of their lives.

One of the reasons I, and most of the manosphere, receive so much scorn from plugged-in, feminine primary society is that we risk to expose this process. This man's story is the inconvenient, but common truth of a pluralistic feminine sexual strategy. Women's capacity to cash out of the SMP, to raise children, to create a semblance of a family life so conflicted with her single life, on what she thinks should be her terms, all rides on keeping men with long term provisioning poten-tial (greater Betas) ignorant of their pre-cuckolding and the conditioning that took so long to convince them would be their responsibility.

"I am so fucking lucky. I got married to a whore, that fucks like a prude."

The primary reason men become preoccupied with women's sexual past is rooted in 'getting the best' she has to offer him sexually. There is certainly more aspects to this (fidelity, secure attachment, etc.), but all men want a slut, they just want her to be *his* slut. Once the belief that he's getting the best sex she has to offer him is dispelled, viscerally and definitively, the nature of the Desire Dynamic (*you cannot negotiate genuine desire*) comes into sharp focus.

There are a great many social conventions prepared to reaffirm a man willing to accept his position of powerlessness in a social order of feminine primacy and open Hypergamy for his participation in fulfilling women's dominant sexual strategy.

The Beta man encountering the newfound attraction a woman's Epiphany Phase presents to him often convinces himself that women's interest in him is genuine and organic. In a sense it is, but although this attraction (not to be confused with arousal) is perceived as genuine on the part of women, it's an attraction born of necessity. That necessity is the need to consolidate on monogamy with a man who'll willingly ignore not just her past Alpha Fucks indiscretions, but participate in what he's been conditioned to believe is his duty as a man from society and start to build a "mature adult" life with her.

A Beta at the Epiphany Phase believes his ship has finally come in and his self-righteous AFC strategy of patience and perseverance will be rewarded.

The social conventions at the time make him believe he's to be more lauded for 'forgiving' a woman's past, irrespective of whether he can *expect* praise for looking past her misgivings.

Getting Her Settled Best

On the Rational Male blog I've had countless men relate to me the experience of having discovered details of their wife or girlfriend's sexual past, and how it surprised them because their wives appetites and sexual freedom with former lovers then has been traded for sexual reservation and self-consciousness with him.

However, this may not have been the experience of discovering a sexual past his wife had no intention of ever allowing him to share with her , but rather the expectation men have of receiving a woman's 'sexual best' in marriage. That may not amount to the sexual experimentation she had in her Party Years, but for a Beta who believes his patience and virtue are to be rewarded after having played "by the rules" for so long, it is an expectation of enjoying the same or better sexual urgency his wife-to-be shared with her past lovers.

That Beta believes it's his turn, because why else would a woman commit to a lifetime investment in a man she didn't think was her best option?

Remember, during the Epiphany Phase a woman's rationale for choosing the Beta for a long term investment is because she's "experienced it all" and finally "knows better than to keep dating the Bad Boys who don't appreciate her." Thus the Beta believes he *must* be, and has always been, the best option for her by virtue of her investment in that belief.

So if she's finally come to realize he's the best option, why would she not expect to enjoy her best sexual performance with him? Especially when he's being told for the first time in his life that his perseverance, dependability and his belief in equalism are what "makes him sexy" now.

For the Alpha Widow marrying the Beta-in-waiting, the comparison of his sexual appeal with prior lovers conflicts with her need to finalize the long term security she couldn't with her previous Alphas (or the men she perceived as Alpha). Thus comes reserved, self-restrained and self-conscious sex with her new Beta provider. She knows that sex with her Beta lacks the intensity and urgency of her prior lovers, but she falls back on her Epiphany Phase self-convinced rationalizations that she's "doing it for the right reasons this time".

That right reason being of course getting pregnant to further consolidate long term provisioning.

Our Beta simply lacks anything really comparable to the same sexual experience as his wife-to-be to know any better (unless of course he finds proof of that experience later), but he gradually suspects her progressive lack of passion, reservations and self-consciousness by comparing it to porn or possibly some of the other women's he's had sex with.

CHAPTER 3

Preventive Medicine

Part III

THE SECURITY &
DEVELOPMENT PHASES

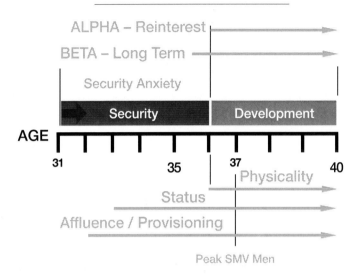

Before I move on in this study I'm going to take a moment to once again clarify the purpose of this time line. It's important to remember that this chronology is meant to serve as a *general* direction for women's maturation and the priorities of attraction they put on men's attributes during these phases of their lives.

By design this graph isn't intended to be a specific outline to account for every woman's individual circumstances, but a somewhat predictable series of phases coordinated with events, behaviors and mental schema that occur during those phases. The perspective I've approached in this outline is one of an unattached (long term single) or semi-monogamous woman with the personal and social options to leverage her sexual agency as well as a subjective degree of control over the direction of her life (or the strong impression that she actually has this control).

Of course, I would be remiss to assume all women's individual circumstances would follow the same series of instances subject to the same set of circumstances.

In any one woman's life there are far too many subjective eventualities to consider that would fit into the scope of this book, which is why I've detailed these phases in as general terms as I can fashion them.

To the point though, it is up to any one Man to determine how a woman's personal conditions, her past decisions and the consequences of her past discretions or indiscretions contribute to what is motivating her along this general outline of life phases. It's entirely possible, if not likely, a woman would have had a prior marriage or be a single-mother during any or all of the phases I've detailed. It's also not unlikely a woman might be a serial monogamist or married during the duration of her Party Years.

The art of determining what motivates a woman according to the phase of life she's in, her socialization and how her circumstances modify or are modified by it is what the 'A' in PUA represents – "Artistry."

The important part of determining what motivates women's behaviors and mindsets is to frame these personal circumstances against this outline of women's life phases. In general, the phases and progression of maturity (socially, personally and biologically), her prioritization of attractive male attributes, and the resulting purpose-driven behaviors don't change much for women as a whole. What changes is the context an individual woman finds them attractive in.

It's when you consider how an individual woman's circumstances work within or against this progression, and how you as a Man can first determine if that woman is worth varying degrees of your investment, that you may better leverage what you know about her conditions and the phase of life she's experiencing to your own, or your mutual, benefit.

I frame individual observations and understandings of specific topics as they relate to both women's stage of life and their circumstance. This has been a part of my writing process since I began making forum posts years ago, but in real life, in the moment, you need to have a basic grasp of who you're dealing with, and what motivates her according to what priorities she places on men and herself at any phase of life – as well as considering the social influences she's being subjected to.

Who cares?

Right now all this probably seems like a lot of effort and a lot of hassle.

"Why the hell even bother Rollo? If I had to untangle a chick's psyche and socialization every time I want a new piece of ass I'd just be a monk."

In truth, on various levels of consciousness, you already make most of theses assessments about a woman when you invest any degree of effort (Game) in her – even if just to get laid.

You may not realize you're doing it. Your investment in a woman is itself modified by your own conditioning, your deficiencies and strengths, but rest assured, you *are* making these assessments on some level of consciousness.

The difference now is that you have an outline to be better aware of the framework you're making these assessments in – that's a cornerstone of Red Pill truth.

Understanding what motivates a woman at any phase of her maturation isn't terribly difficult to grasp – once you yourself have experienced that phase with a woman. And that's the intent of my developing this outline, to help (younger) men without the benefit of this prior, sometimes detrimental, experience make informed assessments about the motivations of women they may be interested in at various stages of their maturity.

Equally important is an understanding of how the social conventions and rationales a feminine-centric society endorses and propagates for women factors in to their own ideologies, as well as how they absolve women's already solipsistic nature from personal accountability as she matures.

Furthermore, what's also important is the understanding of the guilt and regret that results from not having lived up to the expectations these social conventions convince women they should be entitled to have experienced by a certain developmental phase. Women tend to be both the perpetrators and (later) the victims of the same conventions by design.

With the rise of instant communication, only recently have men began to connect the dots with regards to how these social conventions have been established to correlate with the decisions women make for themselves and the fluidity with which these conventions allow them to rationalize the outcome of those decisions.

Hypergamy has always been an impulse for women, but until the sexual revolution's 'liberation' of women from the societal and ideological balances that previously kept Hypergamy in check, there was less need for the many social conventions now necessary to balance women's accountability (psychologically and sociologically) in that new 'freedom'.

The Security Phase

Women's priorities for attraction (not necessarily arousal) are dependent upon the necessities dictated by which phase of life she's currently in.

One reason I tagged men's peak SMV at or around 36-38 is partially due to their relative capacity for attaining the characteristics and accomplishments that women find the most desirable for long term commitment at about the same time women are the most necessitous of those qualities.

As women approach the Epiphany Phase (later the Wall) and realize the decay of their SMV (in comparison to younger women), they become progressively more incentivized towards attraction to the qualities a man possesses that will best satisfy the long-term security of the Beta Bucks side of her Hypergamy demands.

For many women this realization is their first experience with the dread that comes from a new uncertainty of attracting and retaining a man in monogamy.

Too many Blue Pill apologists dismiss the SMV realities my graph depicts by comparing the Party Years desires of an SMV peaked 23 year old girl with the vested value a 37 year old SMV peaked man represents to women's overall, long term, dualistic-need Hypergamy. What maximizes the SMV of a woman in her peak is not equal to what maximizes the SMV peak of men.

During what I term the security phase, women's prioritization of attraction shifts to a man's potential for provisioning.

While the newfound attraction to intrinsic qualities of a man are overtly exaggerated as appealing to women during this phase, it's essentially a man's proven capacity to provide enough resources for himself and a potential mate (and future family) that are key to this attraction. These are qualities an SMV peaked man is socially *expected* to possess, and socially expected to deliver for a woman precisely at the time in which she finds herself the most necessitous of these qualities and provisioning (29-31 years of age).

It is during the security phase women will begin to alter their self-expectations, as well as overtly bemoan their frustrations about their own inability to secure commitment from what they now perceive would be a socially equitable mate.

The social conventions already in place for women in this phase make them comfortable in attempting to shame men into compliance with their long term security needs. This is the phase you will most likely hear a woman complain about "men's fragile egos", men being threatened by 'strong independent women' or some other frustration about men not cooperating with the social script of their rapidly decaying, dualistic sexual strategy.

Settling

Security anxiety and the conflict a woman experiences with her SMV decay forces two outcomes for her; she can convince herself to believe her SMV is still comparative to her intersexual competitors or she can settle on a hypergamously substandard man who'll gratefully embody what the provisioning aspect of her Hypergamy demands. If she's followed the Alpha Fucks schedule during her Party Years it's also possible she finds herself as a single mother seeking a provider to assist in the parental investment her Alpha gene provider wasn't (or is a limited) part of.

I should mention that the Transition and Security phases are a point at which most men's (Betas) feminized conditioning comes to fruition for the Feminine Imperative. The Beta providers who've been patiently awaiting their moment of sexual vindication find their moment of peak attraction – and not uncommonly with the same women (or types of women) who had no use for them during their Party Years.

The well conditioned Beta is nothing if not patient and dutiful in his feminine-primary purpose and it's at this phase he begins to see dividends for his steadfastness in supporting the feminine cause. His willingness to forgive a woman's Party Years' *indiscretions*, he believes, will be an investment in a relational equity any 'quality' woman will appreciate.

It's important to understand that the social engineering of the Feminine Imperative conditions Beta men to be predisposed to this White Knight mentality at precisely the phase women will need his provisioning the most – the stage in which her SMV declines and his begins its ascendancy (as defined by *her* need).

During the Security Phase, affluence, provisioning capacity and the status that should be associated with it become a primary attractant for women. The want for physical appeal and arousal cues are still an important factor in attraction, but indicators of maturity, affluence, and other intrinsic qualities become a priority. That isn't to say a random short term mating opportunity with an arousing Alpha would be ignored (especially around her ovulation cycle), but long term security takes precedence.

Women who consolidate on monogamous commitment during this phase (or in their Epiphany Phase) generally run through a series of mental self-rationalization over their decision to marry the Good Dad, rather than the Good Genes father.

This is an effort women engage in to justify to their consolidating on the security side of their hypergamous sexual strategy. Once children are part of her reality this mental subroutine has to be forced to the periphery of her attentions, but it is a psychological conflict she's either going to resolve by eventually leaving her provider male (and seek out her Alpha Widow substitute) or convince herself and her hypergamous conscience that she has in fact optimized her Hypergamy with the male she settled on.

As a woman matures into her late security phase, and her children become more self-sufficient, it's at this point she becomes more self-critical and retrospective of her Epiphany Phase, and more realistic about her *true* reasonings for experiencing it.

The Development Phase

Because a woman's capacity to attract her hypergamous ideal decays with every passing year, her urgency demands an immediacy with a Man embodying as close to that ideal as possible in the now.

Hypergamy takes a big risk in betting on a man's future potential to become (or get close to becoming) her hypergamous ideal, so the preference leans toward seeking out the man who is more *established* than the next.

The problem with this scenario as you might guess is that women's SMV depreciates as men's appreciates — or at least *should* appreciate. The same Hypergamy that constantly tests and doubts the fitness of a man in seeking its security also limits his potential to consistently satisfy it.

From the Security Phase into the Developmental Phase is generally the time during which a woman has satisfied the security needs side of her Hypergamy (Beta Bucks) with a man she consolidated on a long term security with during her Epiphany-Transition Phase.

Before I elaborate further I should remind men that this particular phase can sometimes precede the Epiphany-Transition Phases for women who, by circumstance (e.g. an unplanned pregnancy), personal conviction, pairing with a man she believes has such future SMV potential, or believes is so far above her own foreseeable SMV (looks, affluence or status/fame) that she feels compelled to consolidate on him.

This early security phase may also be the result of a particularly bad experience a woman in her Party Years had with a prior Alpha lover – the emotional trauma of which convinced her to console herself with an accessible Beta orbiter who was patient enough (and fortunate enough) to be his dutiful, forgiving and supportive self in the right place at the right time.

Most commonly however this phase usually occurs within a 7 to 9 year window just after a woman consolidates on (or should have consolidated on) a long-term security prospect male; and this is usually after her transitioning from her Party Years and dealing with the urgency of finding that prospective male.

It's important to delineate the circumstances which affect women who've successfully paired prior to this phase from the women who remain single, never-marrieds or early divorcers. Between the ages of 27 and 37 these circumstances define how a woman engages and copes with her development and redevelopment phases.

The 7 Year Itch

For this 7 to 9 year stretch in her early to mid thirties, a married woman will likely content herself with some semblance of what feminine-centrism defines for her as domesticity.

That may likely include a working/motherhood role, but for the most part the vestiges of her Party Years usually become something she'd rather not be reminded of, particularly so if she's settled on a provider-male who doesn't excite her the way her former Alpha lovers did, and she gradually tires of his whiney wonderment at why she's not as sexual with him now that they're married with children as she was with those prior Alpha lovers.

There's a very interesting social convention that accompanies this phase for the married woman. In fact, there was an old movie dedicated to it, it's called *The 7 Year Itch*. It was a cute movie, but it was based on a very real psychological phenomenon. The cutesy social convention revolves around men developing a wandering eye for strange vagina after mysteriously being married for 7 (a magic number) years. The reality is that most marriages tend to dissolve at two stages, after the 7 year mark and then again at the 20 year mark.

Primarily this is due to a couple having had at least one child (possibly 2) and after that kid reaches 7 and is becoming more autonomous, men and women do some relationship evaluation.

From a tribal-evolutionary perspective this would be the point at which a child is more or less self-sufficient with a minimum investment on the part of a male, but in contemporary relationships it's also the point at which a woman has had time enough to reevaluate her Epiphany Phase decision to pair with the provider (father of her children or otherwise) and compare his actualized SMV to the idealizations she still holds about past Alpha lovers or Alphas she imagines would succeed him.

Just to be complete, the 20 year mark is generally the point at which both parents become 'Empty Nesters' and a second reevaluation takes place. More on this in Part IV.

The Path to Spinsterhood

For women unable or unwilling to settle, compromise or otherwise consolidate on a long term monogamy, her security phase becomes a personal effort in generating long term security for herself.

This security may come with some help from a generous, feminine-primary state, or with the help of child support and / or alimony from a dissolved marriage, or single-pregnancy prior to this phase, and of course she may entirely ignore the dictates of her "biological clock" (fertility window) and double down on her own feminine-masculinized conditioning by providing it exclusively for herself.

Since Roissy so eloquently outlined this woman's demographic, I'll quote him here with his outline on Gaming 31-34 year old unmarried women:

31 to 34 year olds

In some ways, women in the 31-34 age range are the toughest broads to game. (By "toughest", it is meant "most time consuming".) It's counter-intuitive, yes, but there are factors at work besides her declining beauty which mitigate against the easy, quick lay. For one, it is obviously harder to meet single 31-34 year old women than it is to meet single younger women. Marriage is still a pussy-limiting force to contend with for the inveterate womanizer, but Chateau apprentices are hard at work battling the scourge of mating market disturbances caused by the grinding and churning of the marriage machine.

But the bigger reason 31-34 year olds are harder to game than any other age group of women has to do with the wicked nexus of entitlement and self-preservation that occurs at this age in women. When you combine a disproportionate sense of entitlement fueled by years of feminism, steady paychecks and promotions, and cheerleading gay boyfriends with suspicions of every man's motives and a terrible anxiety of being used for a sexual fling sans marriage proposal, you get a venom-spitting malevolent demoness on guard against anything she might perceive as less than total subjugation to her craving for incessant flattery and princess pedestaling.

[...] "I have an easier time bedding and dating 23 year olds than I do 33 year olds."

This defies all logic until you see it through the eyes of the hamster sweating its fluffy ass off in a woman's brain. (Poor little creature must be pooped out by the mid-30s.) Sure, a 33 year old is not as hot as the 23 year old version of herself, but her ASD (anti-slut defense) is through the roof, as is her self-conception as a hot marriage-worthy commodity. Many older women will tell themselves that their experience, maturity, accomplishments and financial stability mean they should be way more valuable to men seeking wives than some young babe on the take. Of course, they have to tell themselves this because reality isn't making it easy to believe.

These are the kind of women who have sexual flings with college guys, because they can psychologically box those men in as "purely for fun" adventures. But the men the 31-34 year old women really want are the older, established men who will give them a marriage proposal and a family. This is why it is counterintuitively harder to game the older woman who still retains a vestige of her youthful attractiveness: she wants and expects so much more than the younger woman.

Social Conventions

During her Epiphany Phase the Alpha Widow or former cock-carousel riding wife-to-be may convince herself that she actually saw an Alpha potential, or a potential for long term success, in 'settling' on that Beta in the long term.

While I have had men relate horror stories about women knowing that they were settling and being insecure about their futures before or at the time of their weddings, I'm going to suggest that this foreknowledge is rarely a conscious aspect of women's insight. "Turning" on their husband-to-be later in life is rarely a preconceived plan, but it is a predictable outcome for men who persist in a Beta mindset throughout their marriages.

Social conventions abound for women to rely on as they become less incentivized to have sex with their Beta husband after the first child. Body image considerations, 'mismatched libidos' and "well, sex is supposed to taper off after marriage, everyone knows that" are just some of the prepackaged tropes ready for use.

The Turning

Once the first (or possibly second) child arrives, a woman's order of intimate priorities changes or "turns" to that of the child. The sex "reward", the 'cookie time for good boy', for desired behavior or performance 'turns' off, or sex is used as an intermittent reward for desired behavior (doing domestic chores, etc.).

Sex becomes a utility; a positive reinforcer for her Beta's increasing of his provisioning capacity rather than the true, visceral enjoyment she had with her past lovers or possibly the younger version of her husband.

This new functionality that sex represents to a wife becomes a 'turning' on her husband who believed he would always be her most intimate priority. In the instance of a woman marrying her 'Alpha Provider' this may in fact be the case, but that Alpha doesn't have the same concern with, and didn't marry his wife under the same preexpectation a Beta does.

For the man who persists in his Beta mindset (or the guy who regresses into that mindset) this 'turning' becomes more and more pronounced. The turning comes out of the bedroom and into other aspects of their relationship – finances, familial ties, her expectations of his ambitiousness, his asserting himself at work or with their mutual friends – on more and more fronts he's compared to other men and the ghosts of the Alphas she knows or has known.

Even though the Beta is aware his children are now his wife's true priority, his Blue Pill conditioning still predisposes him to sacrifices. Again, he meets with ready-made social conventions that shame his discontent.

"Is sex all that's important to you? It shouldn't be, because it's really what's on the inside that counts", but he can't shake the feeling he's slipping out of her respect.

This is when Beta Dad doubles down. His Blue Pill expectations of himself require an all-consuming, self-sacrificing predisposition. The horse will work harder. His wife may have lost respect for him by this point, but his sense of honor and duty press him on. He doesn't want to be like his own oppressive or non-present father was. He wants to 'out-support' his father's ghost, or what he believes 'other guys' would do when their marriages get tough.

So he waits it out, but she's 'turned' on him by this point. It wasn't planned, but all of his martyr-like determination only makes her that much more resentful for having settled on this Beta. After a certain stressing point, her disinterest or indignation goes even beyond his capacity to stay committed to a losing investment. These are the guys who tell me, "Damn Rollo, where were you when I was 30? I wish I'd known then what I know now."

Do all marriages and relationships follow this schedule?

No, but it's important that men know the signs, understand what's really expected of them and know when they're being settled on despite all a woman's self-interested refutations of that. It's important they realize that performance isn't limited to how well they meet a woman's expectations, but that performance means ignoring those preconceptions and exceeding them because he has a passion to excel on his own, and for himself.

It's important that he lives in his own Frame and that any woman, wife or otherwise, participates in his Frame at his pleasure. Beta men rarely have those expectations because they begin from a position of scarcity and a preconditioned responsibility to forgive a woman's sexual strategy while still being gushingly appreciative that she chose him to settle on. He was told he doesn't deserve a great girl like her and he still believes it.

PREVENTIVE MEDICINE

PART IV

THE REDEVELOPMENT /
REINSURANCE & SECURITY PHASES

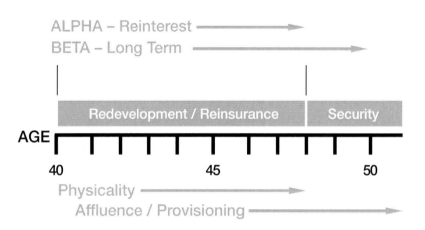

Back when he had a terrestrial show, radio personality Tom Leykis had everyday women call in and tell their stories of how they 'used to be' sexually and how they are now. He came up with this after driving past a grade school on his way to the studio and seeing all of the women there waiting for their kids to come out and wondered about what their lives used to be like in their childless 20s. This was a wildly popular topic and the confessions just poured in as if all of these women had been waiting for years to come clean anonymously about the sexual past that their husbands would never dream they were capable of.

Each of these women sounded proud of themselves, almost nostalgic, as if those experiences were some kind of past accomplishments.

This is why I laugh at the concept of the Quality Woman most men believe are jewels in the rough only they had the good fortune to find. Don't misinterpret that as a "women = shit" binary opinion. I mean it in the sense that most guy's concept of a quality woman is an unrealistic idealization. There's not a guy in the world who committed to monogamy with a woman who didn't think she was 'quality' when he decided to commit to her.

Even if she was a clinical neurotic before he hooked up with her, she still had "other redeeming qualities" that made her worth the effort. It's only afterwards, when the world he built up around his idealization of her comes crashing down in flames, that she "really wasn't a Quality Woman after all."

The Schism

An interesting internal schism occurs for women during the latter half of the first Security phase and through the Developmental phase. The first aspect of this psychological schism is a drive for an unalterable sense of security. As she matures, the priority for an enduring security intensifies with each child she bears and each life incident where that degree of security is tested.

For the married woman who consolidated upon her best available provider male, this intensification usually manifests itself as a ceaseless series of shit-testing, not only over his capacity to consistently deliver an ever increasing need for that provisioning, but also the Alpha suitability she convinced herself that the Beta she married would mature into later. The primary conflict for her during these phases is that her provider male's SMV potential never quite looks like or compares with the idealized memories of the Alpha men she entertained in her Party Years.

I've written several essays regarding the dynamics of the Alpha Widow, but at no other phase of a woman's life is she more prone to mourning a prior Alpha lover than when she enters the Developmental stage.

This is when the security a woman was so incensed to in her Epiphany Phase becomes a liability, but still a necessity of her life. This assured security affords a woman a renewed focus on the Alpha Fucks side of Hypergamy – an Alpha reinterest in physicality and the hope that her maturity would make her a better judge of the type of man who might better fulfill that Alpha role than her current provider.

From a social convention perspective this is the 'cougar' fantasy phase. Unless a man has reinvented himself and capitalized on his SMV potential so significantly as to separate himself from the prior impression of Beta providership 'acceptability' a woman initially expected of him, five minutes of Alpha experience in her 20s will always trump 5-10 years of Beta dedication on his part.

If women can realize the Alpha Fucks aspect of Hypergamy during her Party Years, and then realize the Beta Bucks aspects of Hypergamy after the Epiphany Phase, then the internal schism a woman experiences in her Developmental Phase becomes a difference between her reconciling those two aspects within the man she's currently paired with. The second aspect of this schism is a marked re-interest in the Alpha attributes of either the man she's currently paired with, or the Alpha attributes of men outside that pairing. This side of the schism is particularly frustrating for both Alpha and Beta men paired with a woman experiencing it.

Deal with It

The more an Alpha man actualizes his SMV potential – through maintained (or improved) looks, career, maturity, affluence, status, etc. – the more a woman's need for enduring security becomes threatened as her SMV consistently decays in comparison to his. A woman's logical response to this new form of competition anxiety usually manifests in two ways.

The first being an intense motivation to domineer and control her relationship by placing herself in a dominant role. She assumes (or attempts to assume) headship of the marriage / relationship by way of a new, convenient, conviction or from a self-created sense of her husband's (by association all men's) inherent untrustworthiness bolstered by social conventions that insist women need to be the head of the house (i.e. "she's the *real* boss").

Her insecurity about her own comparative SMV manifests in her demanding he 'do the right thing' and limit his SMV potential for the sake of a more important role as her (and their family's) dutiful provider. The message becomes one of "don't think too highly of yourself mister, you've got a lot of responsibilities to live up to."

Of course the problem with this is that a man acquiescing to such dominance not only loses out on his capacity to maximize his SMV peak potential, but also confirms for his wife that his status isn't as Alpha as he's confident it is. This Alpha disenfranchisement will play a significant part in a woman's Redevelopment Phase.

The second logical response is apathy and resentment. A disconnect from her SMV-peaking mate may seem like a woman's resigning herself to her non-competitive SMV fate, but it serves the same purpose as a woman's insistence for relational dominance – an assurance of continued security and provisioning as the result of his willfully limiting his SMV potential.

This apathy is, by design, paired with the guilt that her mate is more focused on his own self-development than the importance he should be applying to her and any family. The result becomes one of a man chasing his own tail in order to satisfy this passive insecurity and failing passive shit-tests.

In either instance the seeds of a man's success or decline are planted in his ability to identify this schism in relation to how it aligns with his SMV potential at the same time it affects his long term partner.

The problem with the schism is that for all the limitations a woman would emplace against a man actualizing his SMV potential, the same limitations will also constitute a significant part of her justification for being dissatisfied with him during her Redevelopment Phase.

Redevelopment / Reinsurance

The Redevelopment Phase can either be a time of relational turmoil or one of a woman reconciling her hypergamous balance with the man she's paired with. The security side of this hypergamous balance has been established for her long term satisfaction and a new Alpha reinterest begins to grate at the ubiquitous, almost too dependable certainty of that security.

Bear in mind that the source of this certainty need not come from a provider male. There are a lot of eventualities to account for. It may come from a 'never married' woman's capacity to provide it for herself, the financial support levied from a past husband(s) or father(s) of her children, government subsidies, family money, or any combination thereof.

In any event, while security may still be an important concern, the same security becomes stifling for her as she retrospectively contemplates the 'excitement' she used to enjoy with former, now perceptually Alpha, lovers, or perhaps the "man her husband used to be".

My fellow, esteemed blogger Dalrock has long covered the topic of women entering the *Eat, Pray, Love* (after the movie) phase very well, coining the phrase "She was unhaaaaaappy,.." This is the justification call of for women entering the Redevelopment Phase. Divorce-fantasy media abounds for women in this phase.

Depending on when she consolidated on long term monogamy, her kids are at, or almost at an age of real independence. It may even be at the "20 year itch" empty nest stage I described in part three, but there is a fundamental reassessment of the man she's paired with and how his now realized SMV potential has either proved to have been a good bet, or a disastrous misstep. And as with the various prior phases of maturity, she finds there are convenient social conventions already preestablished for her to help justify the decisions she'll make as a result of this reassessment.

The binding, cooperative arrangements of childrearing that necessitated her drive for security gradually decrease in importance, giving way to a new urgency – pairing with someone "she *really* connects with" before her (adjusted for age) SMV / looks are entirely spent on the provider male she now loathes the idea of spending a future with. That Beta has served his usefulness and now she realizes what she really needed all along was a man who she has a true respect for under the conditions which her maturity has at last made her aware of.

This is the turning point at which most Beta men, still hopefully reliant on the false notions of an earned equity in their relationship, find themselves on the sharp end of the feminine Hypergamy they've cognitively dissociated themselves from for a lifetime.

It's not all doom and gloom however. Depending upon a woman's degree of self-awareness and realism about her late-stage SMV, the decision may simply be one of pragmatism – she understands she's with the man who can now best embody a hypergamic balance for her in the long term – or she genuinely has a long term (feminine defined) love and affinity for the man she's paired with, who finally '*just gets it*'.

Other considerations factor in as well; it's entirely possible his SMV peak will endure longer than her reassessment of him will take to determine. Religious conviction may play a (albeit convenient) part in this reassessment, or she may realistically assess her own SMV as decayed to a point where staying with her provider male is her only tenable option.

There's an interesting trend in the divorcing schedules of Baby Boomers that strongly correlate with this Redevelopment Phase reassessment I've described here – it's called Grey Divorce. Americans over 50 are twice as likely to get divorced as people of that age were 20 years ago:

> *Jim Campbell, 55, of Boulder, Colo., says he and his wife grew apart after 34 years together. "The No. 1 best thing in common that my ex-wife and I had was raising kids," Campbell says. When their two sons grew up, he says, "we just didn't have enough activities, passions, interests that were in common. And when the boys were gone, that just became more and more — to me — obvious." – National Public Radio Interview, Grey Divorce*

As is the wont for a feminized media, the focus is on men who divorce their wives, but statistically it's women who initiate over 70% of all divorces. That's an important statistic to bear that in mind when considering the psychological impetus for women's Redevelopment Phase.

In the interest of fairness, a woman can also find herself forced into this Redevelopment as the result of a man who'd come to realize his SMV peak and became actively aware of how a woman's Hypergamy had influenced his decisions for him. There are a minority of men who take the Red Pill or otherwise who exit a marriage they'd been 'settled' on for as her Plan B, or they may in fact want to redevelop themselves for the same reasons women make the reassessment and capitalize on what value their SMV has left to them.

Regardless of how she comes to it, nothing is more daunting for a woman than to reenter the sexual market place at such a severe disadvantage. After the Wall, women dread the idea of having to start over in a sexual market place in which they are grossly outmatched, so even the slightest deviation from the 'security forever' script becomes a major ego threat. If that security is more or less assured, there are feminine social conventions ready to make that prospect more palatable. '40 is the new 30', "you still got it", and of course the strong independent woman® brand offers women a plan for 'cougardom'.

Depending on a woman's relative SMV (that is to say amongst her generation's peers) she may entertain these conventions more or less successfully, but this *reinvention* of a woman's Party Years, still suffers from a need to reestablish a semblance of security after a point. While it may be 'exciting' to relearn how to maneuver in a new SMP, the underlying desire is still one of security.

Late Phase Security

Finally we come full circle and back to a new interpretation of the same security a woman sought after her Epiphany Phase. During this late phase, that may last from a woman's late 40's, 50's or even indefinitely, as a result of an inevitable SMV decay, the security side of a woman's Hypergamy swings into its final, permanent, position. It's important to remind yourself of the distinction that this security isn't necessarily founded on financial provisioning, but rather an emotional, intimate dependence and acceptance for a woman from an acceptably masculine man – often in spite of a past that she would rather be (expects to be) forgiven of by virtue of her age and her perceived life experience.

While she may harbor some desire to live vicariously through the experiences her now grown daughters or younger female friends in various phases themselves, her message to them is one of precaution, but tempered with the subconscious awareness of how Hypergamy has set the frame for her past. This is the phase during which (duplicitously) women tend to mentally rewrite their past for what they believe should be the benefit of younger women.

As an aside, I should point out that with the advent of the internet and the permanency of all things digital, this is becoming increasingly more difficult for mid-life women.

This is the phase during which a woman not only desires secure acceptance of who she is from a suitable man, but it's also the phase she attempts to create a secure social paradigm for herself. To be sure this drive is firmly couched in a woman's innate solipsism, but her desire for security extends beyond a want for her own personal, assured, security, and to woman-kind on whole.

Women in this phase may be concerned for the futures of their daughters – and sons who may come into contact with women following the same hypergamic paradigm she used on their father(s) – but the concern is voiced for society and women as a whole. Rarely is this social concern an admission or testament of her own regret, but rather it's something she must address to reconcile the parts of her past, the undeniable results of her hypergamy, that she can't escape.

Once menopause occurs that retrospective need becomes more urgent.

Social Conventions – Briffaults Law

Robert S. Briffault *(1876 – 1948)* was trained as a surgeon, but found fame as a social anthropologist and in later life as a novelist. You can look him up on Wikipedia to get a better understanding of his social ideas – some I agree with, others I think are dated – however Briffault's Law has found an unlikely popularity in the 21st century manosphere and finds a new relevance when contrasted with the Late Security Phase:

> *The female, not the male, determines all the conditions of the animal family. Where the female can derive no benefit from association with the male, no such association takes place.*
>
> — *Robert Briffault, The Mothers, Vol. I, p. 191*

As you can guess, this proposition makes for an interesting parallel when you consider that a woman has reached an age well past her prime sexual years and has, for the better part, her long-term security needs provided for by family, past or present husbands, social support infrastructures and female-unique social benefits.

There are other additions and interpretations various Red Pill bloggers have applied to this law, but for the purposes of understanding the later maturity phases here I think it's best to stay with Briffault's initial concept.

In 2013 the Pew Research Center released an analysis on marriage trends based data from the U.S. Census Bureau. That analysis indicated that while nearly two-thirds of previously married men expressed a desire to remarry, less than half of previously married women had the same desire.

You can digest that data in the context of our contemporary sexual marketplace and come to the conclusion that women simply aren't prepared for, or willing, to make the effort to secure new monogamy, but I'd propose that much of that lack of will is also the result of Briffault's Law. Men, and particularly men of their own demographic and comparative socioeconomic status, simply don't serve the same usefulness to women who's long term security (both financial and interpersonal) is relatively provided for.

On some level of consciousness women perceive less or no benefit from those men in the same degree to which they had use of them when facing their Epiphany Phase earlier in life.

"He was never much of a man..."

Since I started writing on SoSuave, and especially more now that I've detailed a societal comfort with an open Hypergamy, I've had many guys relate a similar story about how their grandmother, mother or mother-in-law had just openly told him or his wife that her husband was never "much of a man".

These women were all in their late 70s to early 80s and at that phase of life all bets are off. What do they really have to lose by letting their daughters and grand-daughters in on grandma's words of warning about "settling" on a man? I've even had women readers relate how their own mothers confessed that there was "just a part of her she just could never share with a man like her father."

These confessions usually came after her husband was in the ground or had been delivered to the assisted living facility or was too far gone to really register the gravity of her *real* end-of-it-all estimate of him after living the better part of her life with him. The guys who relate these stories to me are Red Pill aware so their jaws dropping came with a little knowing expectation, but imagine how the Blue Pill husband of the daughter of one of these elderly women must process that confession. What mental contortions does a man need to do to fit that information into a Blue Pill mindset?

When a woman has nothing to really lose by copping to it is when they're most comfortable with openly expressing Hypergamy. This is becoming more common for younger women due to the social and personal security they're '*entitled*' to now, but for women who don't really feel that security has solidified until their golden years this admonition and confession of open Hypergamy almost seems like a relief to them. A relief in the hope that they've warned their daughter or granddaughter to opt for monogamy with an exciting Alpha lover/husband (no matter how perceptual) rather than the 'safe bet' she made by settling on her Plan B man, her Beta-dependable husband she conveniently 'found' in her Epiphany Phase.

As women age towards their later years the urgency to warn younger generations of the sisterhood about the results of their hypergamous life decisions becomes more pressing. To be sure, there's a degree of desire to live vicariously through their daughters' and granddaughters' experiences, but more so, this confession is for their own need of closure – a final coming clean about what was really influencing those past decisions and living (or not) with them. There comes a point in a woman's life when admitting the ugly truth feels better than worrying over keeping up the pretense of genuine concern.

Far too many Blue Pill men (even young men) are terrified of living the life of the lonely old man. They imagine that if they don't comply with the Feminine Imperative's preset relational frame of women that they'll live lives of quiet desperation. In the first book I outlined this in the Myth of the Lonely Old Man – the threat point is one where men are encouraged to believe that if they don't comply with women's relational primacy they'll endure a life of decaying loneliness into old age, unloved and devoid of children who'll comfort them bedside as they peacefully pass into the next life.

What these Blue Pill men fail to realize is this is simply one more part of the fantasy they're conditioned for. Do a Google image search for "end of life issues", see all of those pictures of grandpa holding hands with wife and family in a clean comforting hospice bed saying his last goodbyes before he passes on? That advertising is the Blue Pill fantasy. In all likelihood you'll die in an elderly care home, from lung fluid buildup, in the middle of the night with no one around or a complete stranger in the bed next to you. I understand that's a depressing thought, but the truth of it is you really have little pull in deciding how you're going out at that stage, and hopefully that wakes you up about living a Blue Pill existence based on fear, compliance and appeasement to the end.

Put that into perspective with a man who wakes up to his Red Pill conditions.

HIERARCHIES OF LOVE

INTERSEXUAL HIERARCHIES

One of the *withdrawal symptoms* of unplugging from the Matrix of a Blue Pill existence is usually an overwhelming nihilism that results from being torn away from the previous Blue Pill preconceptions a man has been conditioned to for most of his life. It's my hope that in the future Red Pill men will make the necessary interventions and apply what they've learned from their unplugging and Red Pill truths in general towards their sons (and daughters) as well as other men they know or are related to. Unfortunately, until then, the process of breaking away from that conditioning is usually going to begin as the result of a traumatic break-up, a divorce, or having had the relational equity a man thought he'd built a long term relationship on proved worthless in the face of Hypergamy.

It's a sad reality of unplugging that it most often starts as a result of emotional anguish, but to pour salt in those wounds is then having to live with the harsh realities that the Red Pill makes men aware of – that more or less everything they'd held as an ego-investment up to that point was founded on a feminine-primary conditioning. I summed this up in the first book with *The Bitter Taste of the Red Pill*:

> *The truth will set you free, but it doesn't make truth hurt any less, nor does it make truth any prettier, and it certainly doesn't absolve you of the responsibilities that truth requires. One of the biggest obstacles guys face in unplugging is accepting the hard truths that Game forces upon them. Among these is bearing the burden of realizing what you've been conditioned to believe for so long were comfortable ideals and loving expectations are really liabilities. Call them lies if you want, but there's a certain hopeless nihilism that accompanies categorizing what really amounts to a system that you are now cut away from. It is not that you're hopeless, it's that you lack the insight at this point to see that you can create hope in a new system – one in which you have more direct control over.*

Try to keep this last part in mind as you read what I propose in this section. I read a lot of guys in various forums getting despondent after having the Red Pill make sense to them, but that despondency is really a simple lack of not having a path already preset for them to follow. Instead of the easy answers and prerequisite responsibilities that the Blue Pill and the Feminine Imperative had ready for him to follow, now in his new awareness he's tasked with making a new path for himself, and that's both scary and exciting at the same time.

Love Styles

In almost four years of blogging and a book written, my three most popular posts have been the Love series – *Women in Love, Men in Love* and *Of Love and War* (found in *The Rational Male*). Though my SMV graph gets the most link backs, the Love series are easily the most viewed posts on the Rational Male blog. Unfortunately they're often the most misquoted and misunderstood.

One of the toughest revelations of the Red Pill is coming to terms with the difference in experience and concept that men and women apply to love. The core principle in *Women in Love* is usually misunderstood upon first reading. For different reasons, deliberate or otherwise, both men and women critically misunderstand the main premise of that essay:

Iron Rule of Tomassi #6
Women are utterly incapable of loving a man in the way that a man expects to be loved.

In its simplicity this speaks volumes about the condition of Men. It accurately expresses a pervasive nihilism that Men must either confront and accept, or be driven insane in denial for the rest of their lives when they fail to come to terms with the disillusionment.

Women are incapable of loving men in a way that a man idealizes is possible, in a way he thinks she should be capable of.

Most critics of this assessment of how either sex interprets and considers love tend to blow past this last part. They oversimplify my meaning and sputter out something to the effect of, "That Tomassi guy thinks that women can't ever **really** love men, what preposterous crap!"

Of course that isn't my assertion, but I understand the want to dismiss this notion, particularly for men and women invested in the ideal of egalitarian equalism. It's a threat to the ego-investment that men and women are anything less than co-equal and fully rational agents who come together for a mutually agreeable benefit. The simple mechanics of women's innate Hypergamy puts the lie to this presumption, as well as confirms the relevancy of women's constant, qualitative conditionality for whom (really what) they'll love.

I think it's ironic that the same people who disparage this concept are among the first to readily embrace the pop-psychology notion of "*Love Languages*".

I get why this idea pisses off women (and feminized men); it's very unflattering to be accused of loving men from a position of opportunism. However, it's important to understand that I don't make this observation to condemn the way women approach love – although I'm sure it will follow, my point isn't to presume a 'right' or 'wrong' way for women to love men or vice versa. There are beneficial and detrimental aspects of both women's opportunistic approach to love, and men's idealistic approach to love. That said, I happen to believe that the differing ways men and women love each other evolved to be complementary to the other – each sex's strengths compensating for the weakness of the other.

For all the "OMG! I can't believe this Red Pill asshole thinks women can't really love men" misdirection, I should point out that well intentioned men, especially the newly Red Pill, are often guilty of a similar oversimplification.

Theirs is an attempt to find validation in the (usually recent) trauma of having been cut away from their prior Blue Pill conditioning. A similar sentiment of, "Rollo says women can't **really** love men. Of course! It's all so clear to me! Now I know why she left me" satisfies a simplistic need for confirmation of their former condition.

And again, it's not a *right* or *wrong* way of loving – it's the lack of recognizing there is a difference in men and women's concepts of love and being on the punishing side of that lack. Most men will want to apply their concepts of honor or justice in assessing how '*right*' men's idealistic love is, while women will still see the inherent value in loving *what* a man is as a prerequisite for loving *who* a man is.

Hypergamy doesn't care about men's idealistic expectations of love, but neither does men's rationality make concessions for what facilitates women's opportunistic approach to love.

Romantic Souls

I pulled the following quote from a post on The Red Pill subreddit forum:

*My whole life, I've had it nailed into me that I would be able to find **true love** if I was honest and hardworking. As I grew older it was, "If I'm somewhat fit and have a good job making 60k-80k a year, I'll find that beautiful girl that **loves me as I love her**".*

As I've stated on many occasions, it is men who are the True Romantics. Granted, it's the indeliberate result of centuries of evolved 'courtly love', but in the realm of what qualifies as a true act of romance, it's men who are the primary actors; it's men who 'make' (or want to make) romance happen. And of course therein lies the problem, a man cannot 'make' romance happen for a woman.

For all a man's very imaginative, creative, endeavors to manufacture a romance that will endear a woman to him, his 'trying' to do so is what disqualifies his intent.

For every carefully preplanned 'date night' after marriage, there's a college girl swooning to bang her boyfriend living in a shit-hole, sheets over the windows, furniture from the dumpster, pounding shitty beer and sleeping on a soiled mattress on the floor. Romance isn't created, romance just happens, and it's a tough, but valuable, lesson when men come to realize that a happenstance bag of Skittles, or a ring made from a gum wrapper in the right place at the right time meant more to a woman than every expensively contrived 'romantic getaway' he'd ever thought would satisfy her need for lofty romance.

An important part of the Red Pill is learning that the most memorable acts of love a man can commit with a woman are acts of (seeming or genuine) spontaneity and never apparently and overtly planned (and yes, that applies to sex as well).

This is a source of real frustration for a man since his Blue Pill conditioning expects the opposite from him, and his romantic nature – the nature that wants her to "*love him as he loves her*" – conspires with his problem solving nature, thus prompting him to ever greater romantic planning for what he hopes will be an appreciated, reciprocated love.

The Hierarchy

The true source of a man's frustration lies in his misdirected hope that a woman's concept of love matches his own. His ideal is a beautiful girl that loves him the same way he loves her. The presumption (a romantic one perpetuated by the myth of egalitarian equalism) is that his concept of idealized love is a universal one which women share with men in general and him in particular.

Thanks mostly to men's Blue Pill conditioning, what men fail to ever consider is that women's hypergamic based love always considers *what* he is, before she invests herself in *who* he is. This is the root of the intersexual hierarchy of love

The Conventional Model

Before the rise of feminine social primacy, the above 'flow chart' of love prioritization would hardly have been an afterthought for a man. Through any number of evolutionary and sociological progressions, the base understanding of how men's love began from a position of protecting, provisioning for and stewarding the lives of both his wife and children wasn't a concern worth too much of his conscious consideration. Neither was a prevailing desire for a reciprocal model of love the overshadowing concern it is for men today.

To be sure, a baseline requirement of a returned love, sex, respect and fidelity were important elements, but this wasn't the originating basis of male desire for being loved. There was no expectation of a woman *loving him as he loved her* (and by extension their children). To be a man was to have the capacity to provide and sustain a surplus of resources beyond his own provisioning while providing a sense of protection and security.

In the series *Breaking Bad*, an interesting dialog is exchanged between the characters of Walter White and Gustavo when he convinces Walter to cook meth for him in order to ensure the support and security of his family before he dies from cancer.

> *"A man provides, and he does it even when he's not appreciated, or respected, or even loved. He simply bears up and he does it, because he's a man."*

You can look the clip up on YouTube, but Gustavo's monologue seems like an anachronism, especially in the light of a Red Pill awareness of the potential for injustice and the veritable certainty of a provisioning arrangement that will be a one-sided proposition for a man – whether he's loved, respected, appreciated, married or divorced.

Undoubtedly there'll be men reading this bristling at the idea of a non-equitable model for love, but know that this idea of an equitable model is the result of the conditioning that an egalitarian equalism has predisposed men to believe is even possible.

Before the rise of feminine primacy, a man's expression of love through his support and guidance simply weren't things women or children had the capacity to reciprocate. The advent of women's independence, real or imagined, has served to strip men of this core understanding of the differences between male and female concepts of love. In the effort to feminize men more fully, and position men in a condition of confusion about what constitutes masculinity, this concept of love was replaced by a feminine-primary model for love.

While a woman's respect, and a degree of love may flow back to her man, her primary love and concern is directed towards her children.

One reason we're still shocked by women who kill their children (pre or post natal) is due to an inherent acknowledgment of this natural dynamic. Women's brain function and biochemistry largely evolved to predispose them to bonding with their children, and thus ensure the survival of the species. Beyond the rigors of physically gestating a child, raising children to self-sufficiency required a considerable investment of effort and resources – not to mention constant attention. Nature selected-for women with an innate, biological and psychological capacity to nurture and direct love primarily towards their offspring.

The internal psychology women evolved to vet for men who displayed traits for both Alpha physical prowess and parental investment / provisioning potential are a result of children being a one-directional priority for a woman's love. While a degree of maintaining a man's continued personal investment and commitment to the family unit requires her attentions in the form of sex and affections, a woman's primary *love* focus is directed towards children.

Granted, not all women are capable of having children (or some even desirous of them), but even in these instances substitute love priorities still supersede directing her primary attention towards a man. It may seem like I'm attempting to paint women's love as callous or indifferent, but this 'directioning' isn't a conscious or deliberate act, but rather it's due to her innate understanding that a man is to direct his love towards her as a priority.

The Feminine Primary Model

Don't wait for the good woman. She doesn't exist. There are women who can make you feel more with their bodies and their souls but these are the exact women who will turn the knife into you right in front of the crowd.

Of course, I expect this, but the knife still cuts. The female loves to play man against man, and if she is in a position to do it there is not one who will resist. The male, for all his bravado and exploration, is the loyal one, the one who generally feels love. The female is skilled at betrayal and torture and damnation.

Never envy a man his lady. Behind it all lies a living hell.

– Charles Bukowski

For my more optimistic readers, you'll be happy to know I don't entirely agree with Mr. Bukowski's sentiment here, however Charles gives us a great introduction to the next progressions of intersexual hierarchies.

While I'm not sure every woman is as skilled as the next in "betrayal, torture and damnation" as Charles' waxes poetic about, I do believe that his understanding of the male nature is not only accurate, but that same male nature is actually the source of his equating women with betrayal, torture and damnation. It's not that women are inherently evil, it's that men's idealism make them so available to being betrayed, tortured and damned.

If you're at all familiar with Charles Bukowski, you'll know he was one of the last true son's of bitches – the unapologetic epitome of gloriously arrogant self-concern and masculine independence. For what he lacked in polish he made up for in talent and a brutal honesty that could never be acknowledged in the feminine centric social order of today. In the mid 60's he was a feral, instinctually Red Pill Man.

Charles, for all his musing on women, knew that it was the male nature that facilitated women's damaging of men. The feminists of his generation and today simply dismiss him as a relic of a misogynist era, but his real insight wasn't about women, but rather about men's inner workings.

"The male, for all his bravado and exploration, is the loyal one, the one who generally feels love." I'd like to believe that Bukowski was ahead of his time with this, however I think it's more accurate to presume that, due to a constant feminine-primary socialization, men have been conditioned to interpret love in feminine pretexts, rather than acknowledging men and women approach love from different conceptual perspectives.

In light of these differing, often conflicting, concepts of male-idealistic and female-opportunistic love, it's easy to see how a man might find women duplicitous, torturous and damnable – particularly when his feminine 'sensitivity training' predisposes him to believe women share the same love idealism he's been encouraged to believe.

The Feminine Primary model of love is the idealistic fantasy the vast majority of men have been conditioned to presume is a universal model of love. In this fantasy a woman reciprocates that same idealism he has about how she should feel about him based on his masculine-idealistic concept of love. That love eventually must (potentially) include children, but the fantasy begins for him with a woman's concept of love agreeing with his own love-for-love's-sake approach, rather than the performance-based, opportunistic approach women require of men in order to love them.

The best illustration I can apply to this model is found in the very tough lessons taught in the movie *Blue Valentine*. Look this film up on IMDB or Netflix. The plot of this film graphically outlines the conflict that occurs when a man conflates his idealism of the feminine primary model of love with women's opportunistic model of love. That idealism is exacerbated by a feminine-primary conditioning since early childhood which prepares him to expect girls and women will share in it.

When you look at this model objectively you can't help but see the Disney-esque, Blue Pill promise of a mutually reciprocated love. Men being the true romantics predispose themselves to wanting to believe this model is really the only mutually acceptable model. The dispelling of the fantasy this model represents is one of the most difficult aspects of coming to terms with Red Pill awareness – in fact one of the primary reasons men become hostile to the Red Pill is an inability to *imagine* any other possible model.

For most men the dispelling of this fantasy comes after he's reached the 'happily ever after' part of this schema and he realizes the conditionality his wife places on her terms for loving him. Too late he's forced into the realization that women's love model is based upon *what* he is before *who* he is.

While there is a definitive conditionality placed on her love, men don't necessarily expect an unconditional love. It's usually at this stage that men are conveniently expected (or expect themselves) to 'Man Up' and earn a woman's mutually reciprocated love by adopting the male responsibility aspects of the first, conventional model. "A man provides" and for all of his previous equalist conditioning that made him believe a woman would "love him as he loves her" he blames his inability to achieve that idealistic love on himself for not living up to being a "man" deserving of the feminine primary model of ideal love.

What he's really done is convinced himself of accepting a woman's opportunistic model while retaining the idealism he's been conditioned *never* to reject – thereby leaving her blameless in her own concept of love and making him accountable to it.

It's hard to consider this model without presuming a woman's manipulative intent of a man, but let me state emphatically that, for the better part, I believe most women simply aren't specifically aware of the subconscious, instinctual mechanics behind this intersexual hierarchy model.

Through any number of ways women are socialized to presume that their feminine-primary position implies that men should *necessarily* take the life and maturity steps needed to fulfill women's Hypergamy-motivated, opportunistic approach over the course of their lifetime. We like to bemoan this as feminine entitlement, and yes it can get, and is getting more so, abusively out of hand, but this entitlement and expectation originates in women's opportunistic approach towards love.

Men are the "romantics pretending to be realists" and women, vice versa.

The Subdominant Model

Finally we come to male subdominant model wherein a man, by conditioning and circumstance, expects love from a woman as he would from a mothering dynamic.

Often this situation seems to result from an overly enthusiastic belief in egalitarian gender equality and parallelism, but the underlying motivation is really an abdication of masculinity and, by association, abdication of conventional masculine responsibility. There simply is no presumption of a conventionally masculine 'headship' prior to, or into a long term relationship.

These are the men I call *pre-whipped*; men so thoroughly conditioned, men who've so internalized that conditioning, that they mentally prepare themselves for total surrender to the Feminine Imperative, that they already make the perfect

Beta provider before they even meet the woman for whom they'll make their sacrifice. They've internalized a conditioned expectation to acquiesce to a feminine defined frame before any woman accepts him for intimacy.

The social undercurrent of an ideal gender equalism plays an active role in creating these men, and specifically this hierarchical model. Unfortunately, the social and personal illusion of control this model is idealistically based upon is usually overshadowed by the conventional male-dominant / female-submissive expectations of a naturally fluid, complementary love model.

These are the 'house husband' arrangements, and the 'gender is a social construct' relationships. While the hope is one of a realized egalitarian equalism within the relationship, the psychological struggle eventually becomes one of dominant and submissive gender expectations in the pairing.

In an era when Hypergamy has been given free reign, it is no longer men's provisioning that dictates a woman's predisposition to want to be a submissive partner in their relationships. To an increasingly larger degree women no longer depend upon men for the provisioning, security and emotional support that used to be a buffer against their innate Hypergamous impulses. What's left is a society of women using the satisfaction of optimized Hypergamy as their only benchmark for relational gratification.

Men with the (Alpha) capacity to meet the raw, feral, demands of women's Hypergamy are exceedingly rare, and thanks to the incessant progress of feminization are being further pushed to marginalization. The demand for Men who meet women's increasingly over-estimated sense of Hypergamic self-worth makes the men women *could* submit to a precious commodity, and increases further stress on the modern sexual market place.

For all of the mental and social awareness necessitated by this equalist fantasy, men subscribing to this model inevitably fall into a submissive (conventionally feminine) role. Underneath all of the trappings that make this model seem imbalanced is the reversal of conventional roles which place women into the love flow state men are better suited for since their approach to love originates from idealism (and not a small amount of martyr-like sacrifice for that idealism).

The expectation of feminized men then becomes one of women adopting men's idealistic concept of love-for-love's-sake, only to be gravely disappointed when they discover that women simply lack the capacity for it. Essentially this model forces a woman not only to mother her children, but also her husband.

The most common complaint you'll hear from women forced into this conventionally masculine expectation is their resentment of having to "play mommy" for their husband because he's incapable of taking care of himself.

In the beginning of this section I stated that men and women's approach to love was ultimately complementary to one another and in this last model we can see how the two approaches – idealistic and opportunistic – dovetail together. That may seem a bit strange at this point, but when social influences imbalance this conventional complement we see how well the two *should* come together.

When a woman's opportunistic approach to love is cast into the primary, dominant love paradigm for a couple, and a family, that pairing and family is now at the mercy of an opportunism necessitated by that woman's Hypergamy and the drive to optimize it. Conversely, when a man's idealistic approach to love is in the dominant frame (as in the conventional model) it acts as a buffer to women's loving opportunism that would otherwise imbalance and threaten the endurance of that family and relationship.

Arguments about chores, money, sex life, and romance are most common in couples where the woman makes all or most of the family's decisions. Female decision-making status is an even stronger determinant of relationship dissatisfaction than female breadwinner status. Women can handle making more money in a relationship, but they despise being the leader in a relationship.

Argument frequency decreased among female breadwinners if they were not the primary decision-makers.

When a woman's love concept is the dominant one, that relationship will be governed by her opportunism and the quest for her hypergamic optimization. The ultimate desired end of that optimization is a conventional love hierarchy where a dominant Man is the driving, decisive member of that sexual pairing.

CONDITIONING

EARLY EDUCATION

In late 2014 I had a post on Rational Male that began with a picture of a projection screen being presented to a grammar school classroom. This projection was a list of the collected, learned experiences of a group of 9 year old boys who had been conditioned to a self-loathing of masculinity in a feminine-correct social order.

The question, "What I don't like about being a boy" seemed fairly innocuous, but in a feminine-correct social awareness it becomes a litmus test to gauge how well these boys have internalized feminine-correct, conditioned beliefs. The list of offending grievances were:

- Not being able to be a mother
- Not supposed to cry
- Not allowed to be a cheerleader
- Supposed to do all the work
- Supposed to like violence
- Supposed to play football
- Boys smell bad
- Having an automatic bad reputation
- Grow hair everywhere

The list reads like the table of contents from the textbook of exactly what I'd expect from an organized feminine-primary conditioning, however we need to look deeper. It's important to bear in mind that these *uniquely* male attributes are grievances these boys wish they could alter about themselves. These boys believe their lives would be improved (perfected) if they could be less like boys and more like girls. Masculine incorrect, feminine correct.

I'm often criticized of being conspiratorial for my assertion that the Feminine Imperative conditions men from a very early age to accept their eventual Beta supportive role later in life. While this masculine grievance list from 4th grade boys is a good illustration, it's simply one example of the earliest parts of the feminine-correct landscape men are raised not just to internalize, but to evangelize about to other boys / men as well.

One fundamental aspect of coming to terms with our Blue Pill, feminine-primary ego-investments is understanding where they stem from. Every Red Pill aware man I know has run into the frustration that comes from the desire to *help* his fellow man (and a few select women) unplug from what really amounts to a lifetime of conditioning.

This is a tough aspect of the Red Pill for most people to follow. We want to believe we're intelligent, educated individuals with a remarkable capacity to judge, compare and weigh the merits of the ideas presented to us by others. We don't like to think we've been fooled or we haven't considered enough about our beliefs that constitute who we are as people and how those beliefs are part of our personalities.

In most popular stories Beta men may be protagonists, but they're never really heroes. Every movie, that I can remember, that has a Beta as a protagonist has been a comedy; Beta males are good for laughing at – no one actually admires them.

The same situation exists with Beta men you know. If you tell them the truth they'll say you hate women, or you've dated the wrong types of women, or whatever else they can come up with to protect the mental model under which they operate. They're invested in that mental model and they're happy with it; to challenge it is to, almost literally, destroy the world they live in. Not only will how they view the world be destroyed, but how they view themselves will be destroyed as well.

Ego Investments and Denial

The psychological term for this is called 'ego-investment'. I use this term a lot so I think it deserves a bit of explanation.

When a person internalizes a mental schema (see belief) so thoroughly and has become conditioned to it for so long, it becomes an integral part of their personality. So to attack the belief is to literally attack the person. This is why we see such polarization and violent reaction to people's political, religious, inter-social/inter-sexual, etc. beliefs – they perceive it as a personal attack, even when presented with irrefutable evidence that challenges the assertions of their belief.

One common frustration that the Red Pill-aware express is how difficult it is to open their Blue Pill friend's eyes as to why he's not hooking up, why he's not getting dates (or second dates if he is), why he's constantly getting LJBF rejections, etc., and the flaws in what is really ego-investments and conditioned internalizations. As I'm fond of saying, unplugging chumps from the Matrix is dirty work, and this is made all the more difficult when a person is in a categorical state of denial.

People resort to denial when recognizing that the truth would destroy something they hold dear. In the case of a cheating partner, denial allows you to avoid acknowledging evidence of your own humiliation. Short of catching your spouse in bed with your best friend, evidence of infidelity is usually insubstantial. It's a motivated skepticism. You're more skeptical of things you don't want to believe and demand a higher level of proof.

Denial is subconscious or it wouldn't work. If you *know* you're closing your eyes to the truth, some part of you also knows what the truth is and denial can't perform its ego-protecting function.

One thing we all struggle to protect is a positive self-image. The more important the aspect of your self-image that's challenged by the truth, the more likely you are to go into a state of denial. If you have a strong sense of self-worth and competence your self-image can take hits but remain largely intact; if you're beset by self-doubt (a hallmark of Beta thinking), however, any acknowledgment of failure can be devastating and any admission of error painful to the point of being unthinkable. Self-justification arises from the dissonance between believing you're competent, and making a mistake, which clashes with that image.

Therefore we see Blue Pill men tenaciously cling to a moralistic sense of purpose in their methods which is only reinforced by popular culture in our media, our music, eHarmony, our religion, etc. What they fail to realized, and what becomes cemented for them in denial, is that what they believe are their own, indigenous, self-righteously correct beliefs were modified for them by a feminine-centric influence.

This influence began in our most formative years. Our Blue Pill ego-investments were taught to us as part of our earliest socialization.

For women and men steeped in this feminine correct conditioning, just being presented with the possibility that their ego-investment in that correctness is the result of a childhood and young adulthood conditioning that predisposed them to it will seem preposterous because making them aware of it challenges who they are as a person. If you attack the belief you attack the person.

While I was writing this section I got into an exchange on Twitter with a very pro-feminist girl who'd asked me why I thought feminism was anything other than 'equality for both genders'. While I knew that her conditioned ego-investments in feminism would make any real revelation for her impossible, I proceeded to make my case that the latent purpose of feminism was to unilaterally facilitate Hypergamy by removing all constraints on female sexuality while maximally restricting male sexuality.

Needless to say that made her apoplectic. Her simplistic gut-response was some-thing to the effect of "You think feminism is all about limiting dicks?", but it did make me aware that any Red Pill truth I could confront her with was going to offend her preconditioned, feminine-correct sensibilities.

By even suggesting that the better part of western culture is conditioned from its formative years to default to the feminine seems conspiratorial, but as I stated in the prior book, that conditioning isn't the result of some shadowy cabal of feminist social engineers, but rather an evolving social undercurrent that is by far stronger without any kind of centralization. In fact that's what makes this conditioning so endemic – there is no single source to trace it back to.

What makes unplugging so difficult is coming to realize Red Pill awareness in what feels like a *natural* state of feminine deference. Our earliest education teach-es boys to gender self-loathe, while simultaneously teaching an unquestioning, unqualified value of the feminine (Mother, sister, girlfriend, wife). For women, respect is taught to be a presumed given, not earned as it must be among boys.

It's also important to consider that this default respect is an integral part of men's male-as-protector psychological predisposition. Protect mom, protect sister, protect the girls, carry their books home from school and unwaveringly give them the deference their natural weaknesses should afford them, is part of the protectorate mentality boys are both taught and have a natural affinity for.

This aspect of the male mind which predisposes boys to pedestalize girls is really less about respect and more about culling intimate approval from girls (i.e. *The Savior Schema*). It's the first manifestation of male deductive logic in solving the problem of earning a girl's favor.

The Feminine Imperative has learned how to recognize and exploit this natural deference by including it as an integral part of future men's early conditioning.

Pedestals

One of the first things men are made aware of when they come into a Red Pill awareness is their own predisposition to pedestalize a woman they're interested in. When this tendency to pedestalize is paired with a scarcity mentality and a learned soul-mate romanticism, this can develop into a state of ONEitis a man will have for a woman.

This pedestalization is usually the first barrier a man must break in order to move on to other aspects of Game and Red Pill understanding, but it's important to highlight this tendency because it is such a deeply internalized aspect of a man's earliest conditioning. That feminine-primary conditioning plays on his natural protectorate instinct and then pairs this with a subtle valuation of the feminine that always exceeds his own. From that point a boy can extrapolate a woman's intrinsic value in relation to his own capacity to attract a particular woman as a man.

This is really the heart of ONEitis, an unhealthy all-or-nothing devotion based psychosis that distorts a woman's valuation to him beyond all realistic appraisal. Depending on his own valuation to women on whole, this has the potential to exacerbate a scarcity mentality that was also part of his early conditioning.

He'll "never find another girl so fine" and he literally "can't live without her."

Pedestalization conditioning can be learned in the home, but commonly it's school, church, the media, popular culture, an adolescent's peer group and even former Male Spaces conventionally reserved for only boys/men as the feminine influence pervades into them. The Feminine Imperative is the priority, even when it seems the boy's self-importance and arrogance supersedes it.

That's not to say boys don't resist this influence or hold themselves in higher respect in given social contexts, but it is to say that the conditioning influences of the feminine sets the context in which it can be resisted. In other words, those boys' actions are only "incorrect" based on a feminine-primary definition of correctness. Not prioritizing, not pedestalizing girls/women is the incorrect (shameable) behavior.

Early feminine conditioning predisposes boys to ego-invest themselves in becoming men who will prioritize women's wants and needs above their own.

The "Ladies First" response is the conditioned response to any intergender exchange. This then becomes the first germ of a Beta mindset for men – deferring to the feminine part of his intrinsic personality. This deference becomes an unquestioned part of "just who he is."

Chivalry

Much of what men believe is, or was, chivalry is really a bastardized form of the initial concept courtesy of Hollywood and romanticizations. The concept of chivalry play well with our first conditioning of feminine deference.

This chivalry is simply one of many ideologies that was subsumed by westernized romanticism. Chivalry also applied toward things such as not hitting a man while he wasn't looking or attacking a blatantly undefendable inferior, or even a respected, foe.

It was originally intended (in its westernized form) as a code of ethics determined by the Roman Catholic Church to control the otherwise lawless and violent natures of soldiers and knights who, understandably, had a tendency for brigandism in the middle ages. However, there were also similar codes in feudal Japan (i.e. Bushido).

What passes for most people's understanding of chivalry is actually a classic interpretation and bastardization of western romanticism and the ideologies of 'courtly love', which ironically enough was also an effort by the women of the period intended to better control the men of the early and high Renaissance eras. Essentially it amounted to a taming of the over-dominating masculine influence of the time by laying out a system of prescribed appropriate conditions necessary to satisfy a womans access to her intimacy.

Functionally this chivalry became the feminism of its time and indirectly served much of the same feminine interests for women who relied on indirect power.

Like today's push for men to better identify with the feminine, the idea of courtly love was to 'encourage' men to explore their feminine sides with odes of divine expressions of love, offerings of fantastic (often life threatening) feats to prove one's devotion or presenting gifts beyond compare to again prove ones worth and sincerity to the "object" of his desire – hers being the only gauge for acceptance.

The articles of courtly love are actually the inception of our tradition of buying an expensive wedding ring for a woman. And just like the women of today, their behaviors rarely matched their stated intents, but far be it from the objective eye to cast a doubt upon them for fear of social ostracization.

You'll have to forgive me for the history lesson here but it's an important part in understanding the utility that the anachronism of chivalry plays for men's conditioning by the Feminine Imperative today. That conditioning predisposes men to a presumption of, and expectation of, an old-order valuation of women (based on courtly misappropriations of chivalry), while simultaneously affording them with the direct power that feminism insists men also defer to.

The selective old-order chivalric concepts that served women in the past still make for useful tools in honing men's natural predilection for female protectionism. Chivalry is co-opted to defer to the Feminine Imperative as part of men's conditioning.

Within a feminine-distorted ethical, moral definition of chivalry there is an implied reward for exchange of feminine-primary deferent behaviors by men. In this undefined exchange, an unconditional expectation of feminine deference is conflated with men's principle of honor.

Why The Red Pill is Offensive

What women and feminine-conditioned men find offensive about the Red Pill is that it challenges the conditioned ego-investments they depend upon to operate in a feminine primary social order. Women are of course naturally threatened by men becoming too aware of the latent role this order conditions them for and expects them to play to best optimize their sexual selection options and strategy. The more men aware of this strategy, the likelier they are not to cooperate in a strategy that doesn't hold their true best interests.

Conditioned men cling to those investments because they seem like a noble ideal for which they've been trained to expect will be rewarded with mutually shared, mutually acknowledged (hopefully less conditional), love, respect and devotion, but also access, urgency and frequency of "the best sex of their life."

The Red Pill wipes away the hope inherent in that idealism because it more accurately and reliably predicts human behavior than feminism, or that feminine conditioning, ever has for a man. That's a tough, offensive, pill to swallow after a lifetime of ego-investment in a wavering, unreliable or failed drive for the promised rewards of Blue Pill ideals.

That conditioning predisposes men to believing what *should* be true. Even just the objective questioning of feminine primacy beliefs (to say nothing of Red Pill assertions) triggers shock, outrage and disbelief that any *sane* person could ever ask such a question.

EQUALISM

As I stated earlier, what a lot of feminists hate about Red Pill theory is that it simply does a better job of predicting social behavior than feminism ever has. I'd like to think that Red Pill awareness has fundamentally altered (or enlightened if you'd like) intergender interpretations and understanding in a relatively short time, but that would be a mistake.

There's a distinct group of self-evincing Red Pill guys who like to remind us in various forums that it hasn't always been thus. Their story is one of how our forefathers "knew better" with regard to how men and women ought to interact with one another, and essentially spelled this out for future generations in the religious and philosophical texts of antiquity.

While I can't deny the merit of this, I also know that the men of those bygone eras didn't have anything approaching the mass of information and the connectivity men possess today. It's easy to get caught up in the romanticism of the idea that back in some Golden Age of manhood, men knew about the dangers of allowing women's hypergamous natures to run amok.

I'm sure those men knew of the consequences of allowing women to control their fates. I'm sure there were Beta men and cuckolded men as well, but even the most wise Alpha among them could never, for instance, understand the impact that a unilaterally feminine-controlled form of birth control would effect upon a globalized society.

While the sages of manhood-past still have many relevant lessons for the men of today, they simply lacked the compounded experiences and understanding men possess now. Though they undoubtedly were keen observers of human nature and behavior, the greatest thinkers of antiquity simply didn't have an inkling as to the evolved, biological motivators of the sexual strategies our psyches developed in our hunter-gatherer human past.

What frustrates the advocates of this bygone manhood wisdom is that for all of our collective experience and knowledge, for the past sixty or so years, men struggle to come to terms with what that masculinity should mean to them.

For all of the accumulated male experience and relation of it that's led to Red Pill awareness, men still grapple with 'what being a man means to them'.

The Undoing of Men

When I do consults with men of all ages I have to begin from a presumption that these men's concept of masculinity is usually the result of a deliberate attempt by the Feminine Imperative to confuse men about what being a *man* should mean to him.

Even the men who tell me they were raised by the most dominant, positively masculine fathers still suffer the internalized effects of this feminized effort to cast doubt on men's masculinity.

In a recent series of articles National Public Radio attempted to suss out what it means to be a man in the 21st century. I listen to NPR, and while I know bias will always be an inevitable part of any media, I couldn't help but assess what a morass that attempting to define masculinity has become for contemporary men. Each story, each attempt to redefine masculinity, relied on the same tired tropes the Feminine Imperative has been using for men since the start of the sexual revolution.

Weakness, vulnerability, is sold as strength. Submissiveness and compromise to the feminine is sold as "support" and deserving of praise and a reciprocal appreciation (which never manifests in women). Beta is Alpha and Alpha is insecurity, bluster and compensation.

Those are the main premises, and, to a large degree, most Red Pill aware men realize that behavior is the only true determinant of motivation, and reject the feminized, egalitarian-equalist messaging. However, what still surprises me is that this same, deliberate effort to cast doubt on what masculinity *should* be for a man hasn't changed its message or methods of conditioning men to accept this masculine confusion for over 50 years now.

Through the mid 80s and up to now, the idea of anything positively masculine is either ridiculed, cast as misogynistic, or implies a man might be gay if he's too celebratory of his maleness. Since the start of the sexual revolution, any definition of what masculinity truly should mean has been subject to the arbitrary approval of the Feminine Imperative.

In the absence of a clear definition of what masculinity is for men, the Feminine Imperative is free to create as grotesque a straw man of ugly masculinity, or as beatific a feminized model of masculinity, as it needs to serve its purpose.

Useful chivalrous moralism, blurring and distorting conventional masculinity, raising and conditioning men to accept ambiguity and doubt about the security of a '*manhood*' they're encouraged not to define for themselves – all of these are the methodologies employed to ensure a feminine-primary social order.

Equalism vs. Complementarity

Agreeableness and humility in men has been associated with a negative predictor of sex partners. Physical attractiveness and egalitarianism are also negatively related in males.

The problem inherent in applying reciprocal solutions to gender relations is the belief that those relations are in any way improved by an equilibrium between both sex's interests. This bears repeating here:

The Cardinal Rule of Sexual Strategies
For one gender's sexual strategy to succeed the other gender must compromise or abandon their own.

The mistake is applying a humanistic, egalitarian-equalist, ideal to human sexual strategies that evolved over millennium to be complementary to each other, not an equitable exchange of resources to be negotiated over. This is one reason genuine desire cannot be negotiated – this fundamental is rooted in our most primal, complementary understanding of sex.

The point at which egalitarian equalism (the religion of feminism) fundamentally fails is presuming that intergender relations *should* ideally exist in a goal-state of egalitarian equalism and / or a reciprocally equal state of mutually supportive interests.

Hypergamy doesn't care about equalism or reciprocity.

The conventional gender roles evolved to be complementary to each other as betterment of species survival. Women form the most secure emotional attachments to men 1-2 SMV steps above themselves. Why is masculine dominance such an attractive male aspect for even the most feminist of women who'd otherwise plead for equality among the sexes?

What we're observing here is a rudimentary conflict between an internalized humanist idealism (the way equalism teaches things should be) versus evolved, impulsive realism (the way things are).

The doctrine of equalism presumes a *socialized* expectation of being turned-on or attracted to men exemplifying a 'gender equitable', equalist-correct, mindset and the evolved, visceral arousal / attraction to a man exhibiting the dominant characteristic traits of masculine complementarity.

Another example of this conflict can be found in my own essay on 'Choreplay'.

In 2008 the transactional nature of sex-for-equitable-services was an over blown meme. The message then was that men needed to do more feminine-typical chores around the house, and the equitable exchange would be his wife reciprocating with more frequent and more intense sex as a result of his "equitable" participation in that negotiation.

Fast forward to 2013 and now (by the same author mind you):

"Hey, fellas, put down those vacuum cleaners and pull out the lawn mowers."

"Married men may think helping around the house will up their hotness quotient in the bedroom, but what really matters is the type of chore. Heterosexual married men who spend their time doing yard work, paying bills and changing the oil have more sex than husbands who spend their time cooking, cleaning and shopping, according to a new study on the subject of housework and sex."

"Households with a more traditional gender division of labor report higher sexual frequency than households with less traditional gender divisions of labor,"...

So what you see illustrated here, in just the space of 5 years, is the frustration and conflict between an equalist idealized model versus the evolved complementary model of gender relations. It's not about the equitability of like for like exchanges or like for like reward/benefit, but rather the way that equitability is expressed and how it grates against instinctually human expectations of behavior.

Sex differences, biologically and psychologically, didn't evolve for hundreds of thousands of years to be co-equal partnerships based on humanistic (or moralistic) idealism. They evolved into a complementary form of support where the aspects of one sex's strengths compensated for the other's weaknesses and vice versa.

For every behavioral manifestation of one sex's sexual strategy (Hypergamy in females), the other sex evolves psychological, sociological and behavioral contingencies to counter it (mate guarding in males). The ideal state of gender parity isn't a negotiation of acceptable terms for some Pollyanna ideal of gender equilibrium, it's a state of complementarity between the sexes that accepts our evolved differences – and by each individual gender's conditions, sometimes that's going to mean situationally accepting unequal circumstances.

Feminists (and anti-feminist women), humanists, moral absolutists, and even Red Pill men still obliviously clinging to the vestiges of their egalitarian Blue Pill conditioning, will all end up having their ideologies challenged, frustrated and confounded by the root presumption that egalitarian equalism can ever, or should ever, trump an innate and evolved operative state of gender complementarity.

And thus we come full circle, back to a new model of masculinity that is found upon the evolved complementary order and aided by Red Pill awareness.

I have no doubt that it will be an arduous process of acceptance for Blue Pill, masculine-confused men vainly attempting to define their own masculinity under the deliberately ambiguous contexts laid out for them by the Feminine Imperative, but I do (hopefully) believe that Red Pill awareness is already making a positive impact on countering a presumption of equalism that only truly serves feminine primacy.

It'll take time, but with every man utilizing Red Pill awareness to realign his masculine identity and benefit from it, other men will begin to come to the same awareness or else fall off into their own ambiguity.

OPEN HYPERGAMY

CONTROLLING INTERESTS

"When looking for a life partner, my advice to women is date all of them: the bad boys, the cool boys, the commitment-phobic boys, the crazy boys. But do not marry them. The things that make the bad boys sexy do not make them good husbands. When it comes time to settle down, find someone who wants an equal partner. Someone who thinks women should be smart, opinionated and ambitious. Someone who values fairness and expects or, even better, wants to do his share in the home. These men exist and, trust me, over time, nothing is sexier."

— *Sheryl Sandberg, Lean In: Women, Work, and the Will to Lead*

Sheryl Sandberg, the C.O.O. of Facebook, provides us with a unique illustration of the prevailing feminine psychology that's been evolving since the sexual revolution.

In this statement she is blissfully ignorant of her blatant admission of the reality of feminine Hypergamy, but I felt her '*advice*' to women here represents so much more than just a display of her solipsistic ignorance.

For as long as I've butted heads with many obstinate deniers of Hypergamy's influences, on women personally and society on whole, I'm not sure I've read a more damning indictment of Hypergamy from a more influential woman. Sandberg's advice to the next generation of women essentially puts the lie to, and exposes the uncomfortable truth of, women's efforts to deny the fundamental dynamic of dualistic female sexual strategy – Alpha Fucks / Beta Bucks.

Even if you want to argue the evolutionary psychology and biological origins of women's pluralistic sexual strategy, the Feminine Imperative has progressed to the point that the fact is now socially evident; women have come to a point where they're comfortable in openly admitting the truth that Red Pill awareness has been drawing attention to for well over a decade now.

Courtesy of Sheryl Sandberg, the Alpha Fucks / Beta Bucks basis of women's sexual pluralism is now publicly recognized. It's kind of ironic considering that what the manosphere has been trying to make men aware of for years is now being co-opted, embraced and owned as if women had always practiced an open sexual pluralism – incredulous to any man's shock over it.

However, the truth is that a feminine-centric social order can no longer hide the increasingly obvious fallout and consequences of a society restructured to accommodate women as the predominant sexual interest.

Ironically the best spokeswoman to illustrate the dichotomy between both sides of women's Hypergamy should be Sheryl Sandberg – the voice and embodiment of several generations of women raised on the Feminine Imperative and unilaterally unrestrained Hypergamy. So oblivious is Sandberg to her feminine-primary, solipsistic confirmation of Hypergamy that it never occurs to her that men would be anything but accommodating of her life-plan advice for younger generations of women. It never occurs to her that a *"man who values fairness"* would ever reject her (much less despise her) for the duplicity that women's dualistic sexual strategy disenfranchises men of.

So you see, it's not a Red Pill awakening that predisposes men to believing they're 'owed', 'entitled to' or 'deserving' of sex, love, adoration, affection or anything else from women – it's the generations of women like Sandberg who unabashedly exploit the old order conditioning of Beta Bucks men, while expecting them to dutifully accept their open or discrete cuckoldry with Alpha Fucks men – and then tell them that "nothing's sexier" than their complacency in it with a wriggle of their nose.

Sandberg is ignorant of the feminine-primary implications that her statements draw attention to – and I'm still of the opinion that an innate feminine solipsism motivates more and more women to this admission – but it's impossible to ignore the new degree of comfort in which women feel in laying bare their dualistic sexual strategy.

To some significant extent the Feminine Imperative no longer needs to keep the 'Good Genes' / 'Good Dad' dichotomy ugliness a secret from men any longer.

There is a new ambient sense of an assured long-term security in the feminine mind that is predisposing women to prioritize the 'Best Genes' (Alpha Fucks) side of feminine Hypergamy. Sandberg's 'advice' is a vital confirmation of this, however, she tacitly acknowledges a window of opportunity during which women possess a better capacity to pursue this side of Hypergamy.

"The things that make the bad boys sexy do not make them good hus-bands. When it comes time to settle down, find someone who wants an equal partner."

In these two sentences Sheryl (and by extensions the Feminine Imperative) essentially confirms women's pluralistic sexual strategy, my sexual market value graph depicting women's peak SMV and decay, and the first half of the time line of women's phases of maturity.

Selling the Beta

With regards to men, I believe the most salient part of Sandberg's admission is found at the end.

*"These men exist and, trust me, **over time**, nothing is sexier."*

For the better half of the time since the sexual revolution it was necessary for the Feminine Imperative to convince a majority of men that their eventual Beta providership for women was not only their duty, but also a prime aspect of feminine attraction. Under the (pre-sexual revolution) old-order attraction model this may have been the case to a large degree. However after the revolution, and as women's Hypergamy prioritized towards 'Good Genes' (Alpha Fucks) short-term sexual partners, the 'Good Dad' (Beta Bucks) men needed an ever increasing '*sell*' of their own attractiveness by women.

This persistent sell was a necessary element of ensuring a future long-term security for women while pursuing increasingly more short-term breeding opportunities as feminine-primacy expanded into society.

The future 'Good Dads' would need to be patiently waiting out women's "indiscretion years" during their SMV peak, so the sell became an ever-evolving definition of what women found attractive in men based on that old-order model of dependability, patience, industriousness, and every other characteristic that defined a good provider.

The following quote is from *Why Muscularity is Sexy* by *David A. Frederick* and *Dr. Martie G. Hasselton*:

According to strategic pluralism theory (Gangestad & Simpson, 2000), men have evolved to pursue reproductive strategies that are contingent on their value on the mating market.

More attractive men accrue reproductive benefits from spending more time seeking multiple mating partners and relatively less time investing in offspring. In contrast, the reproductive effort of less attractive men, who do not have the same mating opportunities, is better allocated to investing heavily in their mates and offspring and spending relatively less time seeking additional mates.

From a woman's perspective, the ideal is to attract a partner who confers both long-term investment benefits and genetic benefits. Not all women, however, will be able to attract long-term investing mates who also display heritable fitness cues. Consequently, women face trade-offs in choosing mates because they may be forced to choose between males displaying fitness indicators or those who will assist in offspring care and be good long-term mates (Gangestad & Simpson, 2000). The most straightforward prediction that follows is that women seeking short-term mates, when the man's only contribution to offspring is genetic, should prefer muscularity more than women seeking long-term mates.

Strategic pluralism theory is a functional definition of feminine Hypergamy, but what this theory hadn't yet accounted for (at the time it was published) was the necessitousness of women with regards to short-term mating strategies and long-term parental investment opportunities over the course of their various phases of maturity as they aged.

The Beta investment sell was necessary because it ensured male parental investment at a later (usually the Epiphany Phase) time in a woman's life. Thus, Sandberg's praise of men "*who think women should be smart, opinionated and ambitious. [Men] who value fairness and expect or, even better, want to do his share in the home*" will eventually be sexier than the Alpha "*bad boys, the cool boys, the commitment-phobic boys, the crazy boys*" she encourages women to have sex with earlier in life is an excellent example of this sell.

Ironically it's exactly with this sell that women encourage the very transactional nature of sexual relations with men they're screeching about recently. It's the 'Choreplay' fallacy on a meta scale – do more around the house, play into the equalitarian schema women think they need in a provider, support her ambitiousness and opinionatedness and you'll be considered "sexier" and get her *Best Sex* she's been saving just for a guy like this.

Building the Beta

The problem the Feminine Imperative runs into with *selling* the Beta is that as women's "independence" expands this sell becomes less necessary and less effective. Less necessary because women's personal, social and legal long-term security insurances have become almost entirely disconnected from men's direct (not indirect) provisioning. Less effective because men have become increasingly aware of their disenfranchisement of the old-order provisioning model as being something they might equitably be rewarded for with a woman's intimate interest and genuine sexual desire.

As the consequences and repercussions of women's hypergamous priority shift to Alpha Fucks becomes more evident and real for men; and as their capacity and comfort with connecting and relating these shared experiences with other men becomes more widespread, the less effective the sell is for Beta men awaiting their turn to enter into a pre or post Wall monogamy with the women attempting the sell.

Throughout the 70s, 80s and most of the 90s, the sell was effective because men were isolated socially and technologically from each other's relative experiences. From the late 90s onward that isolation has diminished while the societal results of feminine-primacy have become more glaringly, and painfully, evident to men.

In its ever-reinventing fluidity, the Feminine Imperative found it necessary to transition from selling men on being later and later life long-term providers for women into building a generation of men who would *expect* it of themselves to fulfill that role when the time came. These men would be raised and conditioned to be the patient Beta providers women would need once they had followed the Sandberg model of Hypergamy.

These would be the boys / men who would be taught to "naturally" defer to the authority and correctness of women under the auspices of a desire to be an equal partner. These are the men raised privately and created socially to be ready for women, *"when it comes time to settle down, and find someone who wants an equal partner."*

These would be the men ready to expect and accept a woman's proactive cuckoldry of him in the name of being a pro-feminine equal. These are the men raised to accept a socially exposed, proudly open, form of Hypergamy in place of the *selling* of it to an old-order Beta provisioning model.

The Hypergamy Schism

The problem this creates for women becomes one of dealing with the men they need to *sell* a secretive Hypergamy to and the men they *build* to accept an open form of Hypergamy to. The increasing comfort with an open admission of Hypergamy is relative to a woman's capacity to get away with it.

A woman like Sheryl Sandberg has the means to decisively ensure her future independence and long-term security (at least in the financial sense) whether she's married or not. She could very well return to the Bad Boys she found so arousing and advises women to 'date' but never rely on for direct provisioning. As such she's very comfortable in publicly revealing the ins and outs of post-sexual revolution Hypergamy without so much as an afterthought.

While she publicly affirms the *build* model of Beta provisioning (under the guise of equalism) and expects "*those guys will be awaiting you*" this doesn't hold true for a majority of women. Women with affluence enough, or a physical attractiveness sufficient to virtually ensure their future provisioning are much more comfortable with the build-a-better-Beta model than women who find themselves more lacking in this assurance.

The more necessitous a woman finds herself in the sexual marketplace, the more likely she is to deny the mechanics of her own Hypergamy.

A woman less confident in consolidating on her future long-term security (and / or cooperative parental investment) has a much more personal investment in keeping the ugly, duplicitous truths of Hypergamy a secret from men. As such, these women will be more predisposed to misdirecting the men becoming more aware of this truth and relying more on the *selling* model of Beta provisioning.

Needless to say this split between women comfortable in open Hypergamy and women reliant upon secretive Hypergamy is a point of conflict between the *have's* and *have not* women in the sexual marketplace. The more men become aware of women's Hypergamy and strategic sexual pluralism, (through women's open embrace of it or the manosphere) the more pressure the '*have not*' women will feel to also embrace that openness.

Open Hypergamy

It's gotten to the point now that the Feminine Imperative is comfortable in ridiculing men for not *already* being aware of the Alpha Fucks / Beta Bucks dynamic of Hypergamy, as well as ridiculing them for going along with it anyway.

The expectation that men should already know this dynamic and be ready to unconditionally accept it, and commit themselves to it, engenders genuine shock when a man deviates from that script.

In 2014 there was a popular, salacious story about the 'Spreadsheet Guy' who logged his wife's rejecting his sexual advances and her reasoning for doing so. After making this log public and having it go viral on the internet the anger female commenters expressed over his logging his wife's excuses for turning him down sexually was not due to his actions, but rather what those actions represented for the greater whole of men.

Women's indignation over this was rooted in a perceptually Beta man not *already* being aware of the new role he is expected to play. The new order feminine group-think presumes that any guy who follows the old order socio-sexual contract should already know he's been cast as a dutiful, providing Beta — he ought to follow the prepared script and plan to be the guy who responsibly proves he's a 'better man' for having forgiven her sexual indiscretions with prior Alpha's and accepting the role of being relegated to her emotional supporter and hand-holder.

And all of this after she's had her "self-discovery", Epiphany Phase and then knows who "she really is."

Genies and Bottles

This expectation of men being preconditioned to follow a feminine-primary social order is not just limited to women's expectations. We've progressed to the point that Blue Pill men are themselves becoming vocal advocates for this same acceptance of open Hypergamy.

Under the dubious pretense of concern for the general lack of gallant chivalry and Beta Bucks-side provisioning women are entitled to, these watered down 'purple pill' "Dating Coaches" suffer from the same shock and indignation that a woman, somewhere, might not be given her life's due of having a dutiful Beta awaiting to fulfill the provisioning side of her sexual strategy when her SMV begins to decay in earnest.

In a feminine centric social order, even men are required to be strong advocates for open Hypergamy, and ultimately their own proactive cuckoldry. That a woman may be better prepared than most Beta men to provide for her own security is never an afterthought for them – their sales pitch is the same old-order lie that women will reciprocate intimacy for a man's good nature and virtuous respect for the feminine if he'll only accept open Hypergamy.

But Spreadsheet Guy went off the reservation, "how dare he keep track of his wife's sexual frequency!" The general anger is rooted in his 'not getting' the pre-fabricated social convention that sex (for consummate Beta providers) "just tapers off after marriage", but if he would just Man Up and fall back into his supportive, pre-established role, and learn to be a better, more attentive 'man' for his wife, she would (logically) reciprocate with more sex.

For what it's worth, the men women genuinely want to fuck wouldn't keep track of sexual frequency because a woman's dread of missing out on a sexual opportunity with a desirable Alpha is usually enough incentive to ensure frequency. Alpha Men don't complain about sexual frequency, they simply move on to a new woman. Beta's complain about sexual frequency because they are expected to know and accept (now via open Hypergamy) that they will never enjoy the type of sex their women had with the Alphas in their Party Years. Rather, they are led to believe they would get it (and better) if they accept their new role and commit to a woman's provisioning.

Nobody marries their 'best sex ever'

According to a recent study by *iVillage*, less than half of wedded women married the person who was the best sex of their lives (52 percent say that was an ex.) In fact, 66 percent would rather read a book, watch a movie or take a nap than sleep with a spouse.

Amanda Chatel, a 33-year-old writer from the East Village, says, "With the men I've loved, the sex has been good, sometimes great, but never 'best.' It's resulted in many orgasms and was fun but, comparatively speaking, it didn't have that intensity that comes with the 'best' sex.

"I knew [my best sex partner] was temporary, and so the great sex was the best because the sex was the relationship," she adds. "We didn't have to invest in anything else."

As you can see here, the incremental problem that advocates of the 'Man Up and accept your duty to open Hypergamy' meme will find is that reconciling the old-order social contract they need to balance Hypergamy will become increasingly more difficult as example after example like this become more evident and more commonplace.

These 'Dating Coaches' are hocking advice from the perspective of an old-order social contract for men, in order to reconcile the well earned, well deserved consequences women are now suffering as a result of a new-order, feminine-primary social contract that has embraced unrestrained Hypergamy.

Getting the Best of Her

The following was quoted from a popular 'advice' column in 2014. Emphasis my own:

> *Dear Carolyn (Hax):*
>
> *After multiple relationships not working out because **both parties were dishonest** in one way or another, I decided to use a new approach to my current relationship. I am 23, met my current boyfriend (also 23) online, and decided to be **COMPLETELY HONEST.***
>
> *This was meant to mostly cover my feelings, as **I tended to hold things in unhealthily, but I let it fold over to all aspects, including the disclosure of my sexual history**. I have now learned this was a mistake.*

Not to make any Beta leaning guy even more depressed, but I read this and couldn't help but see how the Sheryl Sandberg 'Open Hypergamy' model is only going to aggravate more and more unplugged, Red Pill aware Betas.

Consider how disenfranchised that dutiful Beta is going to be when he is flat out told to his face by a woman – a woman he was conditioned to believe would appreciate his unique old order appeal – that he'll never be getting the 'sexual best' he believed his wife would have waiting for him in marriage.

It's one thing to read article after article detailing the triumphant aspects of a new open Hypergamy, and it's one thing to see it blatantly used in commercial advertising, but it's quite another to experience it firsthand, viscerally, in your face.

Besides the fact that she's had multiple "relationships" at age 23, I find it interesting that today's woman recognizes this 'openness' as a mistake. Not a mistake with regards to her own choices, but rather the mistake is in feeling comfortable enough to lay bear her sexual strategy for a guy who she expects should already be "accepting of who she is."

In feminine-primary society men are constantly and publicly demonized as the 'manipulator' sex.

The default presumption is to assume men are the one's to watch out for. Men are the sex with the most dishonest nature, with the most to gain sexually by playing games to trick women into believing they're something they're not in order to fuck them and leave them.

This presumptions is really a generalized, meta social convention that builds a foundation for more specific social conventions women need in order to exercise feminine-primary control with men and culture on whole. It's actually a rudimentary convention that's easy to accept for women since feminine Hypergamy has evolved a subconscious 'vetting' mechanism into most women's psyches.

While it's giggly fun and entertaining for women to categorize men into Cads and Dads, the irony of their doing so is that this only highlights women's life-long patterns of deception and the manipulation efforts necessary to effecting their own dualistic sexual strategy.

That sexual selection 'firmware', the one which predisposes women on a limbic level to evaluating mating options of short term breeding opportunities (Alpha Fucks) with parental investment opportunities (Beta Bucks), is the same mechanism that made women the more deceptive sex when it comes to sexual strategies. The problem now is that this hypergamous deceptiveness is being replaced with 'complete honesty' from a macro-societal level down to an interpersonal one.

Ironically, it will be the most stubborn of Blue Pill Beta men, advocating for a return to an old-order social contract, who are destroyed by the very women they hope will respond to it; who will be the last to finally accept and respond to the new-order of open Hypergamy.

CHAPTER 8

BOOK II

SUPPORT WORKS

REJECTION & REGRET

"There's not a lot of money in revenge" – Inigo Montoya

Either directly or indirectly, I wrote a lot about rejection in *The Rational Male*. Usually this is due to rejection, and the fear of it, being the root cause of so very many mental schema, behaviors, rationales, etc. for guys. The chapter *Buffers* from the first book outlines many of these rationales and conventions used to deaden or minimize the impact of rejection, but it's rejection, and how one accepts it, that makes for a healthy or unhealthy response to it.

I wish I could claim authorship of this, but an enigmatic member of the SoSuave forum, *Pook*, had it right – **Rejection is Better than Regret.**

However, for all the wisdom in that simple truth, applying it, learning from rejections and accepting rejection is what primarily trips men up.

I use men exclusively in this context because, for the better part of your life as a Man, based on gender alone, you will experience rejection far more than any woman ever will. If that sounds like a bold statement let me clarify that – you should experience rejection more than any woman.

In sports, in your career, in education, in personal relations, and with the opposite sex, you will statistically experience more rejection than a woman. That understanding isn't intended to wave the male power banner, or make Men the champions of virtue. Neither is it to presume women don't experience rejection themselves; it is a simple observance of fact that rejection is an integral aspect of being male. Get used to it.

So, rejection is preferable to regret, we get that. What we don't get is how to accept and deal with that rejection. I'm not going to type away here and pretend that I have it figured out yet, however I can tell you how men, boys, Betas, and even PUAs will refuse to accept and/or deal with that rejection.

Habits and mindsets that constitute buffers are how men prevent rejection, not how they deal with it once they're experiencing it. But just as men (and women) employ rationales and conventions to prevent or blunt a potential rejection, so too have they developed coping strategies, rationales and techniques that afford them the least amount of discomfort when they have been rejected – or in the case of women, when they are delivering that rejection.

Remember, rejection isn't limited to just inter-gender instances. In fact that's almost a more interesting aspect; your reaction to being rejected for a potential job will be far more measured than if you were rejected for intimacy with a woman. One reason we go to such great lengths to buffer ourselves against rejection is the fear of having to experience it, but often the fear of it is more debilitating than the actual experience.

Revenge

I mention revenge in particular because it's easily the most common, and potentially the most damaging reaction men have with rejection. This can be from enacting something petty and annoying to the actual murder of the rejecting woman. This is the "how can I get back at her?" response, and while it may seem satisfying to 'teach her a lesson' trust that this lesson will never be taught by revenge, no matter how justified or deserving she is of it.

Indifference, not revenge, speaks volumes.

The very consideration of revenge is a waste of your time and a waste of your effort that would be better spent learning and bettering yourself from that rejection. I can personally relate a story of a young man who was just released from prison. He killed the boyfriend who his 'soul mate' replaced him with when he was 16 by stabbing him 32 times. That was his revenge. If he'd been 2 years older he would've been put to death or served a life sentence. You may not be that extreme in pursuing a course of revenge, but the consequences are similar. For as long as you consider revenge, no matter how petty, you'll still be attached to the emotions of that rejection.

Accept the rejection, move on, rejection is better than regret – literally in this case.

Men aren't being prepared, aren't being raised to be Men. In the manosphere we constantly belabor this to the point that we make it a matter of personal pride and duty to instruct our fellow men less fortunate to realize it. Dealing with rejection is the lynch pin to this.

When I read posts from Men I'd otherwise consider Red Pill aware contemplate how best to enact their 'revenge' upon a woman who refused his approach, or in retaliation to a woman's infidelity, I wonder if they are as enlightened as I gave them credit. In facing rejection, you have no choice but to accept it. How you'll do so is a matter of your character.

It's important to cultivate an almost third-person approach to accepting rejection. For a lot of people, particularly those unaccustomed or new to deep personal rejection this is a tough order – and particularly so for men just beginning to put what they've learned of the Red Pill into practice. We get emotionally invested and that's never conducive to making good decisions, especially for men who'd do better to rely on rationality and pragmatism. And we're particularly susceptible to that emotionalism when we're adolescents and young adults with a more limited capacity for thinking in abstracts.

It's part of the human condition to desire what we think is justice. It's our nature to make comparisons, and in the instance of inequality, to see them corrected. And although we rarely consider the ultimate consequences of our actions, this isn't the reason we should temper a desire for revenge. The thing we ought to consider is the overall efforts and resources necessary in order to exact revenge and weigh them against the things we might achieve for our own betterment by redirecting them to our own purposes. Even the efforts required for a slight revenge are better spent with concerns of our own.

This might seem like a long-winded way of saying "Living well is the best revenge", and to a degree I think that's true, but beware the 'Well-lived' life spent in pursuit of revenge.

Revenge should never be your motivation for success. Even the time and mental effort needed to consider some appropriate way of making a woman aware of how she made you feel are resources better spent on meeting new prospective women who will reciprocate your interest. The root of confidence is developing, recognizing and acknowledging as many personal options as possible. Any effort you'd expend on revenge is a wasted opportunity to better yourself. Indifference to detractors and personal success are a far better *revenge* than any one sided injury you could inflict on them in return.

3 Stories

One of my favorite ways of helping young men understand how unimportant their immediate concerns are over rejection is to put things into a larger perspective. When you're in the moment and unable to see the forest for the trees, rejections seems so crushing. It's when you look at things in terms of how they play out in the course of time you realize that instead of some horrible soul-destroying rejection you really dodged a bullet that would've radically altered the progression of the better person you become.

When I was 15 or 16 I was in total love (teenage lust) with this girl named Sarah. I did everything in the AFC handbook to get with this girl – 'played friends' with her after a LJBF ("lets just be friends") rejection, wrote to her, called her all the time, etc. I got the "I'm not ready for a relationship now" line right before she had hot monkey sex with one of my best friends.

He was the Alpha Bad Boy and she couldn't get enough of him even after he'd dumped her, and I of course played right along. Flash forward to when I was 22. I had gotten my shit together, I was in the gym religiously, I played in a very popular band in the area and I was walking through the outdoor halls of the college I attended when I heard some girl's voice say "Rollo, hey!" I looked around and literally looked right past her at first wondering who was calling for me. Then she says, "Hey it's me Sarah." I look down, and sitting on this bench is this 300+lbs morbidly obese woman with the barely recognizable face of this girl I'd obsessed over about 6 years earlier.

I was floored. Apparently she'd gone through rehab for a cocaine addiction and ballooned after it because she replaced the drug with food. For the first time in my life I was speechless.

My second story was about this one girl Bridget who I also had a major Beta crush on in high school and I lacked even the confidence to really approach.

I self-rejected and disqualified myself horribly with her.

Again, flash forward to about 22 and I pull this exact same girl in a club (who actually still looked pretty good), only now I can't keep her off of me. I ended up turning her into a fantastic booty call after the first night. This girl would literally knock on my window and climb in through it to fuck me in the morning before I left for class.

However, later, it got to the point where I dumped her, because she insisted on never taking birth control while reassuring me she was and I thought I had a close call with her being pregnant,…that and I was tapping 4 or 5 other girls at the time that I thought were better plates to spin (even though I didn't know what plate theory was then). The lesson learned; What I couldn't get in high school ended up my left-overs just 5 years later.

Lastly, I had my first 'real' girlfriend look me up online once. This was the girl I first had sex with at 17 and I ended up moving to the college town she was enrolling into so I could keep fucking her. I basically altered the course of my life for 2 years to accommodate her life decisions, only to have her cheat on me and break up with me after I'd moved.

She was my '*first*' so like a well conditioned Beta I naturally assumed she was the ONE, and the better I "supported" her the more she'd appreciate me (i.e. fuck me), so I took it pretty hard. I had still tapped her once or twice after all this, but she dropped off my world for over 20 years.

In my late 30's I get this email from her. I guess she'd looked me up. I checked out pictures of her on a vanity site she had (not Facebook), and I can't say time had been kind to her. At 37 she looked about 55, made about $32K tutoring kids how to read (after that terrific degree I moved to 'help' her get), she's "married" to another woman (an open lesbian marriage I was told). It was kind of an eerie feeling just barely being able to make out the girl I'd known at 17, now at 37.

In all of these situation, but particularly this one (after 20 years), it's hard not to feel more than a little self-satisfied and think karma's a bitch, but I wonder how many women I'd been rejected by who are doing better now after the years. I'd also like to think that men tend to do better with age, but I know this isn't always the case. Though I'm aware that living well is the best revenge, I think that living well in order to exact that revenge is misguided. Things like this will happen regardless so long as you put the emphasis on your own betterment.

Rejection is better than regret.

Keep this in your mind, particularly if you're a younger reader. There are no real failures in rejection, only opportunities to learn. In fact it's your unexamined successes and acceptances that will be more of a challenge to learn from when you're in the middle of relishing them. We tend not to consider what created our successes as carefully and as insightfully as we do our rejections.

It's better to accept a rejection that be tied to a regret you succeeded at.

Our great danger is not that we aim too high for lofty goals and fail, but we aim to low for mediocrity and succeed.

THE BURDEN OF PERFORMANCE

Men are expected to perform.

To be successful, to get the girl, to live a good life, men must do. Whether it's riding wheelies down the street on your bicycle to get that cute girl's attention or to get a doctorate degree to ensure your personal success and your future family's, Men must perform. Women's arousal, attraction, desire and love are rooted in that conditional performance. The degree to which that performance meets or exceeds expectations is certainly subjective, and the ease with which you can perform is also an issue, but perform you must.

One of the most fundamental misconceptions plugged-in men have with regard to their intersexual relations with women is the issue of performance. Back in late March of 2014 I read an interesting article from manosphere blogger *Roosh*. His premise in that post was that men are nothing more than clowns to the modern woman and it struck me that although I certainly agreed with him in the context he presented it, there was more to the 'entertainment' factor than simple amusement on the part of women.

> *"In our contemporary world, women no longer seek out comfort or stability in men as they used to — they seek entertainment. They seek distraction. They seek hedonistic pleasure. This is why provider men (beta males) are so hopelessly failing today to secure the commitment of beautiful women in their prime, and this is why even lesser alpha males fail to enter relationships with women beyond a few bangs. Once the entertainment or novelty you provide her declines—and it inevitably will—she moves on to something or someone else. In essence, the only way you can keep a girl is if you adopt the mentality of a soap opera writer, adding a cliffhanger to the end of each episode that keeps a woman interested when being a good man no longer does."*

After reading this I tried to imagine myself being a recently unplugged man or a guy just coming to terms with the uncomfortable truths of the Red Pill and learning that all of the comforting *"just be yourself and the right girl will come along"* rhetoric everyone convinced me of had been replaced by a disingenuous need to transform oneself into a cartoon character in order to hold the attentions of an average girl.

That's kind of depressing, especially when you consider the overwhelming effort and personal insight necessary in realizing Red Pill awareness. Roosh later tempered this with other posts and although he clarifies things well in Game terms, the root of the frustration most guys will have with the 'clown factor' is that, in these terms and in this context, their performance isn't *who* they feel they are.

In this environment it's easy to see why the MGTOW (men going their own way) movement seems like an understandable recourse for Red Pill men. It's a very seductive temptation to think that a man can simply remove himself from the performance equation with regards to women. I'll touch on this later, but what's important here is understanding the performance game men are necessarily born into. Like it or not, play it or not, as a man you will always be evaluated on your performance (or the convincing perception of it).

I think what trips a lot of men up early in their Red Pill transformation is sort of a sense of indignation towards women that they *should* have to "be someone they're not" and play a character role that simply isn't who they are in order to hold a woman's interest. In some respect women are like casting agents when it comes to the men they hope will entertain them.

Women's prerequisite "character" role they expect men to perform changes as their own phases of maturity dictates and their SMV can realistically demand for that phase. In other words the "characters" they want performed in their Party Years will be different than the ones they want after their Epiphany Phase, which may be different than the character they want for their midlife years.

How realistic it is for men to be that character becomes less and less relevant as women are socialized to expect disappointment from men actually living up to the characters they're conditioned to believe they should realistically be entitled to at various stages of their maturity.

Living Up

Right about now I'm sure various male readers are thinking, "fuck this, I'm gonna be who I am and any girl who can't appreciate me for *me* is low quality anyway." This will probably piss you off, but this is exactly the Blue Pill mentality most *'just be yourself'* Betas adopt for themselves.

It's actually a law of power to despise what you can't have, and deductively it makes sense, but the fact still remains, as a man you will always be evaluated by your performance.

So even with a 'fuck it, I'll just be *me*' mindset you're still being evaluated on how well 'you are just *you*'.

The simple fact is that you must actually *be* your performance – it must be internalized. In truth, you already are that performance whether you dictate and direct that, or you think you can forget it and hope your natural, undirected performance will be appreciated by women (and others), but regardless, women will filter for hypergamous optimization based on how well you align with what they believe they are entitled to in a man in the context of their own perception of their SMV. That perception is modeled upon what phase of maturity a woman finds herself in.

Looks, talent, tangible benefits and other core prerequisites may change depending on the individual woman, but to be a man is to perform. Even if you're a self-defined man going his own way who enjoys escorts to fulfill his sexual needs, you still need to perform in order to earn the money to enjoy them.

It Doesn't Get Easier, You Get Better

For Men, there is no true rest from performance. To believe so is to believe in women's mythical capacity for a higher form of empathy which would predispose them to overriding their innate hypergamous filtering based on performance.

Women will never have the same requisites of performance for themselves for which they expect men to maintain of themselves. Hypergamy demands a constant, subliminal reconfirmation of a man's worthiness of her commitment to him, so there is never a parallel of experience.

Women will claim men "require" they meet some physical standard (i.e. performance) and while generally true, this is still a performance standard men have of women, not one they hold for themselves. There simply is no reciprocal dynamic or prequalification of performance for women, and in fact for a man to even voice the idea that he might qualify a woman for his intimacy he's characterized as judgmental and misogynistic.

Social conventions like this are established to ensure women's hypergamous sexual strategy is the socially dominant one. Expecting a woman to perform for a man is an insult to her 'prize status' as an individual that feminine-centrism has taught her to expect from men.

From a humanist perspective there's a want for a rational solution to this performance requirement, but appeals to women's reason are no insulation against the subliminal influences of Hypergamy.

I've read the works of many a 'dating coach' who's approach is complete honesty and full disclosure in the hopes that a like-minded, co-equal, co-rational woman will naturally appreciate a man's forthrightness, but this presupposes a preexisting equal playing field where subliminal influences are overridden by mutual rationalism.

The real hope is that women will drop their innate hypergamous performance requisites in appreciation of this vulnerable, inadequate honesty.

What they sweep under the rug (and what I'll elaborate on later) is that you cannot appeal to a woman's reason or sentiment to genuinely forgive a deficit in a man's performance. Love, reason; both demand a preexisting mutual appreciation in a common context, but neither love nor reason alleviate the necessity of performance for a man.

Women simply have no incentive to compromise Hypergamy on their own accord. They will not be reasoned into accommodating a situation of mutual needs by overt means.

It is a Man's capacity to perform and to demonstrate (never explicate) higher value that genuinely motivates women to accommodate mutual needs in a relationship, not communication or reasoning – whether that's a same night lay or in a 50 year marriage.

Demonstrating Higher Value

I get the impression that demonstrating higher value tends to get a bad rap both from Blue Pill critics as well as Red Pill aware men. A lot of that gets wrapped up in Pick Up Artist technique and practice. It's easy to dismiss this concept as posturing or bluster, but DHV, as a principle isn't defined by egotistical measures or how well a guy can 'showboat' himself around women.

Much of what constitutes a demonstration of higher value for men is casual and unintentional. In fact the best, most genuine forms of DHV are exhibited when a Man doesn't realize he's actually performing in a way that demonstrates his higher value. This can be as simple as walking int a room in the right context or environment. Evident social proof and a confirmed status he takes for granted is DHV. Even humility can be DHV in the proper context.

What I'm driving at here is that after reading all of this you might think I'm saying you need to be superhuman to qualify for women's performance standards, and again that's kind of depressing – that's not what I'm getting at.

A woman's performance standards are dependent on many varied contexts and according to the priorities she places on the type of character she finds both arousing and attractive and according to what her maturity phase conditions dictate for her.

In many instances it's not *how* you perform so much as *that* you perform.

Ambition and personal drive to perform and be the best and most successful *you* that you can be may have absolutely nothing to do with your intention of attracting a woman, but you are still performing and you will be evaluated on that performance.

Demonstrating higher value or demonstrating lower value is performance whether intentional or not. You cannot remove yourself from this performance equation. You can cease to direct your part in this performance, but until you die you cannot exit the game.

VULNERABILITY

One of the most endemic masculine pitfalls men have faced since the rise of feminine social primacy has been the belief that their ready displays of emotional vulnerability will make men more desirable mates for women.

In an era when men are raised from birth to be "in touch with their feminine sides", and in touch with their emotions, we get generations of men trying to 'out-emote' one another as a mating strategy.

To the boys who grow into Beta men, the ready eagerness with which they'll roll over and reveal their bellies to women comes from a conditioned belief that doing so will prove their emotional maturity and help them better identify with the women they mistakenly believe have a capacity to appreciate it.

What they don't understand is that the voluntary exposing of ones most vulnerable elements isn't the sign of strength that the Feminine Imperative has literally bred a belief of into these men.

A reflexive exposing of vulnerability is an act of submission, surrender and a capitulation to an evident superior. Dogs will roll over almost immediately when they acknowledge the superior status of another dog.

Vulnerability is not something to be brandished or proud of. While I do believe the insight and acknowledgment of your personal vulnerabilities is a necessary part of understanding yourself (particularly when it comes to unplugging oneself), it is not the source of attraction, and certainly not arousal, that most well conditioned Beta men believe it is for women.

From the comfort of the internet, and polite company, women will consider the 'sounds-right' appeal of male vulnerability with regard to what they're supposed to be attracted to, but on an instinctual, subconscious level, women make a connection with the weakness and submission that vulnerability represents.

A lot of men believe that trusting displays of vulnerability are mutually exclusive of displays of weakness, but what they ignore is that Hypergamy demands men that can shoulder the burden of performance. When a man openly broadcasts his vulnerableness he is, by definition, beginning from a position of weakness.

The problem with idealizing a position of strength is in thinking you're already beginning from that strength and your magnanimous display of trusting vulnerability will be appreciated by a receptive woman. I strongly disagree with assertions like those of various 'life coaches' that open, upfront vulnerability is ever attractive to a woman.

The idea goes that if a man is truly outcome-independent with his being rejected by a woman, the first indicator of that independence is a freedom to be vulnerable with her. The approach then becomes one of "hey, I'm just gonna be my vulnerable self and if you're not into me then I'm cool with that."

The hope is that a woman will receive this approach as intended and find something refreshing about it, but the sad truth is that if this were the attraction key its promoters wish it was, every guy 'just being himself' would be swimming in top shelf pussy. This is a central element to Beta Game – the hope that a man's openness will set him apart from 'other guys' – it is common practice for men who believe in the equalist fantasy that women will rise above their feral natures when it comes to attraction, and base their sexual selection on his emotional intelligence.

The fact is that there is no such thing as outcome independence. The very act of your approaching a woman means you have made some effort to arrive at a favorable outcome with her. The fact that you'd believe a woman would even find your vulnerability attractive voids any pretense of outcome independence.

Hypergamy Doesn't Care About Male Vulnerability

In the Rational Male I described men's concept of love as 'idealistic'.

Naturally, simple minds sought to exaggerate this into "men just want an impossible unconditional love" or "they want love like they think their mothers loved them." For what it's worth, I don't believe any rational man with some insight ever expects an unconditional love, but I think it's important to consider that a large part of what constitutes his concept of an idealized love revolves around being loved irrespective of how he performs for, or merits that love.

From *Of Love and War, The Rational Male*:

We want to relax. We want to be open and honest. We want to have a safe haven in which struggle has no place, where we gain strength and rest instead of having it pulled from us.

We want to stop being on guard all the time, and have a chance to simply be with someone who can understand our basic humanity without begrudging it. To stop fighting, to stop playing the game, just for a while.

We want to, so badly. If we do, we soon are no longer able to.

The concept of men's idealistic love, the love that makes him the true romantic, begins with a want of freedom from his burden of performance. It's not founded in an absolute like unconditional love, but rather a love that isn't dependent upon his performing well enough to assuage a woman's Hypergamous concept of love.

Oh, the Humanity!

As the true romantics, and because of the performance demands of Hypergamy, there is a distinct want for men to believe that in so revealing their vulnerabilities they become more "human" – that if they expose their frailties to women some mask they believe they're wearing comes off and (if she's a mythical "quality woman") she'll excuses his inadequacies to perform to the rigorous satisfaction of her Hypergamy.

The problems with this 'strength in surrender' hope are twofold.

First, the humanness he believes a woman will respect isn't the attraction cue he believes it is. Ten minutes perusing blogs about the left-swiping habits of women using the Tinder app (or @Tinderfessions if you like) is enough to verify that women aren't desirous of the kind of "*humanness*" he's been conditioned to believe women are receptive to.

In the attraction and arousal stages, women are far more concerned with a man's capacity to entertain her by playing a role and presenting her with the perception of a male archetype she expects herself to be attracted to and aroused by. Hypergamy doesn't care about how well you can express your humanness, and primarily because the humanness men believe they're revealing in their vulnerability is itself a predesigned psychological construct of the Feminine Imperative.

Which brings us to the second problem with 'strength in surrender'. The caricatured preconception men have about their masculine identity is a construct of a man's feminine-primary socialization.

The Masks the Feminine Imperative Makes Men Wear

To explain this second problem it's important to grasp how men are expected to define their own masculine identities within a social order where the only correct definition of masculinity is prepared for men in a feminine-primary context.

What I mean by this is that the *humanness* that men wish to express in showing themselves as vulnerable is defined by feminine-primacy.

For the greater part of men's upbringing and socialization they are taught that a conventionally masculine identity is in fact a fundamentally male weakness that only women have a unique 'cure' for. Over the past 60 or so years, conventional masculinity has become a point of ridicule, an anachronism, and every form of media from then to now has made a concerted effort to parody and disqualify that masculinity. Men are portrayed as buffoons for attempting to accomplish female-specific roles, but also as "ridiculous men" for playing the conventional 'macho' role of masculinity. In both instances, the problems that their inadequate maleness creates are only solved by the application of uniquely female talents and intuition. Women are portrayed as being the only solution to the problem of maleness.

Perhaps more damaging though is the effort the Feminine Imperative has made in convincing generations of men that masculinity and its expressions (of any kind) is an act, a front, not the real man behind the mask of masculinity that's already been predetermined by his feminine-primary upbringing.

Women who lack any living experience of the male condition have the calculated temerity to define for men what they *should* consider manhood – from a feminine-primary context. This is why men's preconception of vulnerability being a sign of strength is fundamentally flawed. Their concept of vulnerability-as-strength stems from a feminine pretext.

Masculinity and vulnerability are defined by a female-correct concept of what *should* best serve the Feminine Imperative. That feminine defined masculinity (tough-guy ridiculousness) feeds the need for defining vulnerability as a strength – roll over, show your belly and capitulate to that feminine definition of masculinity – and the cycle perpetuates itself.

Men are ridiculous posers. Men are socialized to wear masks to hide what the Feminine Imperative has decided is their true natures (they're really girls wearing boy masks). Men's problems extend from their inability to properly emote like women, and once they are raised better (by women and men who comply with the Feminine Imperative) they can cease being "tough" and get along better with women. That's the real strength that comes from men's feminized concept of vulnerability – compliance with the Feminine Imperative.

It's indictment of the definers of what masculinity ought to be that they still characterize modern masculinity (based on the 'feels') as being problematic when for generations our feminine-primary social order has conditioned men to associate that masculinity in as feminine-beneficial a context as women would want.

They still rely on an outdated formula which presumes the male experience is inferior, a sham, in comparison to the female experience, and then presumes to know what the male experience really is and offers feminine-primary solutions for it.

True vulnerability is not a value-added selling point for a man when it comes to approaching and attracting women. As with all things, any incidental display of your vulnerability is best discovered by a woman through demonstration –never explaining those vulnerabilities to her with the intent of appearing more human as the feminine would define it.

Women want a bulwark against their own emotionalism, not a co-equal male emoter whose emotionalism would compete with her own. The belief that male vulnerability is a strength is a slippery slope from misguided attraction to emotional codependency, to overt dependency on a woman to accommodate and compensate for the weaknesses that vulnerability really implies.

I know a lot of guys think that displays vulnerability from a position of Alpha dominance, or strength can be endearing for a woman when you're engaged in a long term relationship, but I'm saying that's only the case when the rare instance of vulnerability is unintentionally revealed. Vulnerability is not a strength, and especially not when a man deliberately reveals it with the expectation of a woman appreciating it as a strength.

Vulnerability is not Game.

At some point in any relationship you will show your vulnerable side, and there's nothing wrong with that. What's wrong is the overt attempt to parlay that vulnerability into a strength or virtue that you expect that woman to appreciate, feel endearment over or reciprocate with displays of her own vulnerability for.

A chink in the armor is a weakness best kept from view of those who expect you to perform your best in all situations. If that chink is revealed in performing your best, then it may be considered a strength for having overcome it while performing to your best potential. It is never a strength when you expect it to be appreciated as such.

THE CURSE OF POTENTIAL

One of the most frustrating things I've had to deal with in this life is knowing men with incredible potential who, for whatever reason, never realize it (or as fully) because they deliberately limit themselves due to a Beta mindset . Whether it's potential for success due to a particular talent, the potential of their socio-economic state and affluence, or simply dumb luck that put them into a once-in-a-lifetime opportunity, their Blue Pill ignorance or pride, or rule-bound duty to the Feminine Imperative thanks to their Beta frame of mind, hold them back from really benefiting from it.

God forbid you'd have to cooperate with a guy like this in a business or creative endeavor where your own livelihood might be attached to his inability to move past his Beta frame or his feminine conditioning. One of the benefits of becoming Red Pill aware is a heightened sensitivity to how the feminized world we live in is organized; and part of that sensitivity is becoming a better judge of Beta character and avoiding it, or at least insofar as minimizing another man's liabilities as a Beta to how his malaise could affect you.

I used to work with a very rich man who owned a few of the liquor brands I became involved with in my career. While he was wealthy and had a certain knack for developing some very creative and profitable products, the guy was a deplorable chump with regards to his personal and romantic life. He was very much a White Knight Beta bordering on martyrdom when it came to his wives and the women in his life, who were all too happy to capitalize on this very obvious flaw. At one point he was attempting to launch a new product for which he needed some financial backing, but simply couldn't get it from investors because they weren't convinced their part of his venture wouldn't end up as part of his next divorce settlement since he was planning his third marriage.

His self-righteous 'love conquers all' White Knight idealism chaffed at the suggestion he would need a prenuptial affidavit for anyone to even chance being involved with him professionally, but his proven Beta mindset was a liability to his realizing his full potential. His story is an exceptional illustration of this Beta limitation dynamic, but there are far more common examples with everyday men I know, and you probably do too. That limitation may not even be recognizable until such a time that it becomes an impediment to some future opportunity that opens up to you.

Social feminization and the Feminine Imperative both play an active role in curtailing a man's potential, but more often than not it's with a willing male participant. It's important for Red Pill Men to remember that the Feminine Imperative is more concerned about women's perpetuated long-term security than it will ever be about Men actualizing their true potential – even when it means his sacrificing that potential to sustain her security, and by doing so makes him progressively less able to sustain it.

Women who read my Appreciation essay in The Rational Male, trying to wrap their heads around my assertion that women will never appreciate the sacrifices men will readily make to ensure a feminine-primary reality, never take this equation into account. They think I'm attacking the sincerity of their commitment by pointing out a less than flattering truth — Hypergamy wants the security of knowing (or at least believing) that a woman is paired with the best man her SMV merits, but the fundamental problem is that her Hypergamy conflicts with his capacity to develop himself to his best potential.

Turnkey Hypergamy

Hypergamy wants a pre-made Man. If you look back at the comparative SMP curve at the beginning of the time line, one thing you'll notice is the peak SMV span between the sexes.

Good looking, professionally accomplished, socially matured, has Game, confidence, status, decisive and "*Just Gets It*" when it comes to women, ideally characterize this peak. Look at any of the commonalities of terms you see in any '*would like to meet*' portion of a woman's online dating profile and you'll begin to understand that Hypergamy wants optimization and it wants it now. Because a woman's capacity to attract her hypergamous ideal decays with every passing year, her urgency demands immediacy with a Man embodying as close to that ideal as possible in the now.

Hypergamy takes a big risk in betting on a man's future potential to become (or get close to being) her hypergamous ideal, so the preference leans toward seeking out the man who is more made than the next.

The problem with this scenario as you might guess is that women's SMV depreciates as men's appreciates — or at least should appreciate. The same Hypergamy that constantly tests and doubts the fitness of a man in seeking its security also limits his potential to consistently satisfy it.

Developing Potential

The blog *Just Four Guys* had an interesting article on quantifying sexual market value:

> *Rollo Tomassi at Rational Male has a differing graph of SMV based on his personal estimation. While his evaluation of female SMV with age matches both these graphs quite closely, the same cannot be said of male SMV. However, the difference is that he is measuring potential SMV, rather than actual SMV, and he believes that older men who maintain a proper lifestyle can maximize their SMV to far higher levels than younger men can.*
>
> *By age 36 the average man has reached his own relative SMV apex. It's at this phase that his sexual / social / professional appeal has reached maturity. **Assuming he's maximized as much of his potential as possible, it's at this stage that women's hypergamous directives will find him the most acceptable for her long-term investment.** He's young enough to retain his physique in better part, but old enough to have attained social and professional maturity.*
>
> *Thus, what we're seeing here is the SMV that is actualized by the average male, whereas Rollo's SMV is what a man **could** theoretically achieve with good inner game.*

I bolded the salient parts of this because one misinterpretation I diligently tried to avoid in estimating men's relative SMV is in using sex (or the capacity to attract potential sex partners) as an exclusive metric for evaluating men's overall SMV. Sexual notch count in and of itself is not the benchmark for SMV, rather it is a Man's actualization of his real potential (of which notch count is an aspect) that determines his SMV. Hypergamy wants you to fulfill your best potential (the better to filter you), but it doesn't want to assume the risk of protracted personal investment that your fulfilled potential will eventually place your SMV so far above her own that you leave her and her investment is lost.

This then is the conflict between male potential and feminine Hypergamy. I detailed this in The Threat:

Nothing is more threatening yet simultaneously attractive to a woman than a man who is aware of his own value to women.

On a Blue Pill reddit forum I read a criticism of my SMP graph, dismissing it by stating that an early to mid-thirties guy was far more likely to look like your average schlub, with an average low wage job than some mature, successful guy, who's kept himself in shape and maintains some GQ lifestyle.

I have to say I'm inclined to agree; most men, average men, are men who haven't realized the potential they could. Whether this lack is due to motivation, the limitations of a feminine socialization, or an inability to come to terms with their blue-pill reality, they never actualize the potential that would make them higher SMV men. The Blue Pill redditors can't see that it's Men's potential that sets them apart on the SMV scale.

I think that the primary lesson of Game is that one needs to have a life and purpose that makes a man happy and determined to wake up every morning. Once a man takes control of his life, then a woman becomes an interchangeable part of it like anything else. The road to that state only lies through relentless self-improvement and the shedding of prior limitations. Otherwise, the same brutal cycle repeats itself.

DREAM KILLERS

Women should only ever be a compliment to a man's life, never the focus of it.

How common it is today to be married or getting married before we've realized any of our potential. For all the articles I've read moaning about what a listless generation of "kidult" males we've inherited, that's far removed from the reality of the young men I do consults with. No, what they want is just enough Game knowledge to connect with their *Dream Girl* and relax into a blissful beta cocoon of monogamy. They *want* to commit. Their lifetime Beta psychological conditioning makes commitment an urgency for them.

It never ceases to amaze me when I talk with these young men in their teens and 20s and they go to lengths to impress me with their fierce independence in every other realm of their lives, yet they are the same guys who are so ready to limit that independence and ambition in exchange for dependable female intimacy. They're far too eager to slap on the handcuffs of monogamy, rather than develop themselves into men of ambitions and passions that women naturally want to be associated with.

The truth however is that the longer you remain uncommitted, the more opportunities will be available to you. It's been stated by wiser Men than I that women are dream-killers – and while I agree with this, I'd say this is due more to the man involved, and his own complicity and apathy, than some grand scheme of women.

It's actually in women's best interest that you don't commit to them for a variety of reasons. I realize how counterintuitive that reads, but in your being so readily available you decrease your value as a commodity to them.

Scarcity increases value, and particularly when the reason for that scarcity is something that serves another's interest (hers in this example). The mid-20s Man pursuing his ambition to become an attorney in law school or the premed intern spending long hours at the hospital with aspirations of becoming a doctor is hindered and encumbered with the complications that maintaining a monogamous relationship necessitates of him. His time and efforts need to be applied toward achieving his goals to become an even higher value Man – not just in terms of financial success but for his own edification and confidence. Needless to say, the constraints and obligations that maintaining a monogamous relationship require – both in time and emotional investment – make achieving these ambitions far more difficult.

I tend to promote the idea that Men should be sexually and emotionally non-exclusive until age 30, but this is a minimal suggestion. I think 35 may even serve better for Men. The importance being that as a Man ages and matures in his career, his ambitions and passions, his personality, his ability to better judge character, his overall understanding of behavior and motivations, etc., he becomes more valuable to the most desirable women and therefore enjoys better opportunity in this respect.

Women's sexual market value decreases as they age and it's at this point the balance tips into the maturing Man's favor. It's the Men who realize this early and understand that bettering themselves in the now will pay off better in the future, while still enjoying (and learning from) the opportunities that come from being non-exclusive and noncommittal, make him a Man that women will compete for in the long term.

In your mid-20s you are at the apex of your potential with regards to the direction you will influence your life to go. I'm not going to make any friends by pointing this out, but what pisses off most "serial monogamists" is the unspoken regret of having assumed the responsibilities of what monogamy demands *before* they truly understood their potential.

If you are single at 35 with a moderate amount of personal success, you are the envy of most men because you possess two of the most valuable resources men your age or older statistically do not – time and freedom.

I envy you. You are unshackled by the responsibilities, liabilities and accountabilities that most men your age in marriages, long term relationships (LTRs), with children, or recovering from divorce must contend with daily. Without any intention you are in such a position that you can go in any direction of your choosing without considering the impact of your choice for anyone but yourself. Many other men, even in the most ideal of LTRs, do not have this luxury.

When you think of all the responsibilities that are required of most men (and women) in modern life today, you have won the lottery!

I was once asked what I'd buy if money were no object, to which I answered, time. Power isn't financial resources, status or influence over others; real power is the degree over which you control your own life, and right now you are powerful. Trust me, this is as good as it gets and this is made all the better because you are old enough to understand and appreciate what is really at work here.

Women are just damaged goods to you now? So what? You have the freedom to sample as indiscriminately or as particularly as you choose. Can't find a good LTR? Why would you want to? Let her find you. You fear you'll end up old and lonely? I'd fear ending up so paralyzed by a fear of loneliness that you'd settle for a lifetime of controlling misery in a passionless marriage.

I'm an adherent of the 'build it and they will come' school of thought in this regard. Women should only ever be a compliment to a man's life – never the focus of it.

Is it better to choose the path of least resistance to get to an idealized, prefabricated intimacy or self-develop and get the same intimacy? True, both instances put women as the focus of a Man's life, and this is a position that most women will find endearing at first, but suffocating in the end.

Women want to '*want*' their men. Women want a Man who other men want to be, and other women want to fuck. She doesn't want a slave to her intimacy since this puts her in the masculine role. Rather, she wants a decisive mature man who has the confidence to put her off, to tell her 'No', in favor of his ambition and passions as this serves two purposes.

First, it sets his direction as the one of authority and his development as the primary; the results of which she and her potential children will benefit from. Secondly, it puts her into a position of chasing after him – essentially his legitimate ambitions and passions become the 'other woman' with which she must compete for his attention.

Note that I stated 'legitimate' ambitions here. A woman involved with a law student or an intern who have the potential to become lawyers and doctors are fairly solid bets for future security. An artist or musician, no matter how talented or committed to their passions will only be viewed as beneficial if they can prove their case to select women. However this can be offset by single-minded determination, once again, with select women with a capacity to appreciate this.

This said, think about the fellow who's chosen to be a plumber or a mechanic as his calling. The best plumber in the world is only going so far unless he has dreams to own his own business.

All of this is limited by a man's attitude towards the opposite sex. Women are dream killers. Not because they have an agenda to be so, but because men will all too willingly sacrifice their ambitions for a steady supply of pussy and the responsibilities that women attach to this.

So yes it is better to develop yourself rather than take the path of least resistance. That's not to say don't date or enjoy women until you're out of college, in your 30s and have your career in order. It is to say don't consider monogamy until you are mature enough to understand it's limitations and you've achieved a degree of success to your own satisfaction according to your ambitions and passions. It is also to say that women should compliment and support your plans for your own life.

MENTAL POINT OF ORIGIN

Self-Concern Without Self-Awareness

In the first book people thought I was crazy to hold up a guy like Corey Worthington as the example of an 'Alpha Buddha', but there are other examples of the same unpracticed, self-unaware, mojo as Corey.

Personally, I was at my most Alpha when I didn't realize I was. That's not Zen, it's just doing what came natural for me at a point in my life when I had next to nothing materially, only a marginal amount of social proof, but a strong desire to enjoy women for the sake of just enjoying them in spite of it.

Some of the most memorable sex I've had has been when I was flat broke (mostly). It didn't matter that I lived in a two-room studio in North Hollywood or had beer and mac & cheese in the fridge – I got laid and I had women come to me for it.

It didn't take my *doing* anything for a woman to get laid or hold her interest.

All I did was make myself my mental point of origin. It's when I started putting women as a goal, making them into more than just a source of enjoyment, that I transferred that mental point of origin to her and I became the necessitous one.

A lot of guys will call that being 'needy', and I suppose it is, but it's a neediness that results from putting a woman (or another person) as your first thought – your mental point of origin. I use this term often so I thought it deserved a bit more explanation.

Your mental point of origin is really your own internalized understanding about how you yourself fit into your own understanding of Frame. If you haven't read the first book or need a refresher, Frame is the first Iron Rule of Tomassi:

Iron Rule of Tomassi #1

Frame is everything.
Always be aware of the subconscious balance of who's
frame in which you are operating.

Always control the Frame, but resist giving the impression that you are.

If Frame is the dominant narrative of a relationship (not limited to just romantic relations), your mental point of origin is the import and priority to which you give to the people and/or ideas involved in that relationship. It is the first thought you have when considering any particular of a relationship, and it's often so ingrained in us that it becomes an autonomous mental process.

For most of us our understanding of that point of origin develops when we're children. Kids are necessarily "selfish", sometimes cruel and greedy, because our first survival instinct is to naturally put ourselves as our mental point of origin. Only later, with parenting and learning social skills do we begin to share, cooperate, empathize and sympathize as our mental point of origin shifts to putting the concerns of others before our own.

Young boys are generally very Alpha because of this unlearned self-importance. Their innate disruptiveness and pugnaciousness is the source of the almost zen-like, mater-of-fact Alpha bearing of a Corey Worthington. As I stated in the first book, he's not a 'man' anyone might aspire to be, but he is Alpha without intent or self-awareness.

There is a 'first thought' balance we have to maintain in a pro-social respect in order to develop healthy relationships. The problem we run into today is one in which boys are (largely) raised to be the men who provide more than they need in order to establish a future family. That learned, conditioned, mental point of origin is almost always focused outward and onto the people he hopes will reciprocate by placing him as their own point of origin.

Natural feminine solipsism makes this exchange a losing prospect. Women are both raised and affirmed by a vast social mechanism that not just encourages them to put themselves as their mental point of origin, but it shames and ostracizes them for placing it on someone or something other than themselves.

By now I'm sure that much of this comes off as some encouragement towards a retaliatory selfishness or narcissism, but putting oneself as his own point of origin doesn't have to mean being anti-social or sociopathic. It requires a conscious decision to override an internalized understanding of oneself, but by placing yourself as your mental point of origin you are better positioned to help others and judge who is worth that effort.

It often requires some emotional trauma for men to realign themselves as their own point of origin, and I feel this is a necessary part of unplugging, but the real challenge is in how you deal with that trauma in a Red Pill aware state. If you are to kill the Beta in you, the first step is placing yourself as your mental point of origin.

So there are some things you'll want to ask yourself:

Is your first inclination to consider how something in your relationships will affect you or your girlfriend/wife/family/boss?

When men fall into relationships with authoritarian, feminine-primary women, their first thought about any particulars of their actions is how his woman will respond to it, not his own involvement or his motivations for it. Are you a peace keeper?

Do you worry that putting yourself as your own first priority will turn a woman off or do you think it will engage her more fully?

Are you concerned that doing so may lead to your own form of solipsism, or do you think 'enlightened self-interests' serves your best interests and those with whom you want to help or become intimate with?

GAME CHANGERS

Whenever I consult teenage guys or young adult men I'm always reminded about how my 'Game' has changed over the course of my lifetime. The 17 year old Rollo Tomassi would be appalled at the mindset of the 46 year old Rollo Tomassi.

Granted, much of that shock would probably be attributed to the lack of experience my younger self had with regards to female nature, human nature and, if I'm honest, I suffered from the same naiveté most young men do when it comes to judging people's character. In fact, at the time, my belief was that I shouldn't ever judge anyone's character, nor did I, nor should anyone really, have the right to.

Part of that assumption was from an undeveloped religious learning, but more so it was due to a youthful idealism I held – I'd been conditioned to believe not only that you "can't judge a book by its cover", but also that you shouldn't do so, and ought to be ashamed for considering it.

I'm flattered that people might think I'm some phenomenal interpreter of psychology, the nature of women, intergender relations and a model upon which men should aspire to in order to get laid and still have a great (now 18 year) marriage. It has not always been so.

If I have any credibility now it's not due to my getting everything miraculously right, but because I had everything so horribly wrong more often than not.

One of the most valuable lessons I learned in my time studying psychology and personality studies is that personality is alway in flux. Who you are today is not who you will be in another few years. Hopefully that's for the better after learning something and applying it towards your own personal progress, but it could equally be a traumatic experience that changes you for the worse.

For better or worse, personality shifts – sometimes slowly, sometimes suddenly – and while you may retain aspects of your personality, mannerisms, talents, past experiences and beliefs into the next iteration of yourself in a new phase of your life, rest assured, you will not be who you are *now* at any other time.

Game Beyond PUA

I'm sorry if this sounds all fortune cookie to you at the moment, but it's a necessary preface to understanding how Game changes for men as their life situations and circumstances change during different phases of their lives and the shifts in their own personalities and learned perceptions change as they age.

It's an easy step for me to assume that, were I to find myself single tomorrow, I wouldn't approach Game in any degree as I would were I the 26 year old version of myself. Indeed, the primary reason I've involved myself in expanding the Preventative Medicine series into this book is to help men at different phases of their own development understand what to expect from women *and* themselves during these periods of their life.

Game, for lack of a better term, should be a universal knowledge-tool for the everyman. Game and Red Pill awareness is (should be) a benefit for men regardless of their circumstances or station in life.

Game and Red Pill awareness is applicable for men of every social or personal condition – even the short, pudgy guy who empties the trash in your office. He may not have the potential to enjoy sex with a swimsuit model, but the tenets of Game can help him improve his life within his own circumstances.

When I was writing *The Rational Male* I specifically wrote and published a post on the *Evolution of Game* to be included in the book in order to demystify an impression of Game which I still think people (particularly the Blue Pill uninitiated), sometimes intentionally, misconstrue as some magical panacea to their 'girl problems'. My definition was thus:

> *For the unfamiliar, just the word 'Game' seems to infer deception or manipulation. You're not being real if you're playing a Game, so from the outset we're starting off from a disadvantage of perception. This is further compounded when attempting to explain Game concepts to a guy who's only ever been conditioned to 'just be himself' with women and how women allegedly hate guys "who play games" with them. As bad as that sounds, it's really in the explanation of how Game is more than the common perception that prompts the discussion for the new reader to have it explained for them.*

At its root level Game is a series of behavioral modifications to life skills based on psychological and sociological principles to facilitate intersexual relations between genders.

Game has more applications than just in the realm of intergender relations, but this is my best estimation of Game for the uninitiated. Game is the practical application of a new knowledge and increasingly broader awareness of inter-gender relations – often referred to, for convenience, as Red Pill awareness, by myself and others in the broader manosphere. Game begins with Red Pill awareness and using that awareness to develop Game.

"The body of infield evidence collected by 15 years of PUA is far more reliable and valid than anything social science has produced on seduction"

– Nick Krauser (krauserpua.com)

As I've written in the past, everyone has Game. Every guy you know right now has some idea, methodology or system of belief by which he thinks he can best put himself into a position of relating to, and becoming intimate with, a woman.

From even the most rank Beta plug-in to the 14 year old high school freshmen boy, every guy has some notion about what he, and by extension all men, should do in order to become intimate with a girl. I described this a bit in *Beta Game* where I outlined the Beta plan of identifying with women's "needs" and adopting a feminine-primary mental point of origin in order to become more like the target(s) of his affection.

What 'formalized' Game comes down to is what genuinely works for the betterment of his life. Men don't seek out the manosphere because their Beta Game works so well for them.

I'll admit, this was my own Game when I was in my late teens. Like most properly conditioned young men, I subscribed to the idea that men needed to be more empathetic and sensitive to women's experience (rather than putting priority on his own) as the most deductive means to getting a girlfriend who'd appreciate my uniqueness for being so 'in tune' with the feminine.

If you'd have asked me at the time (the mid 80's), my belief was that the best way to 'get the girl' was to take women at their word, use their "advice", be their friend, make her comfortable, sacrifice your own (chauvinist) self-importance and support her importance, and mold your incorrect male self into a more perfect feminine ideal. The idea was that the lesser you made yourself, the more you made of her, and the more likely she was to reciprocate intimacy in appreciation.

That was my Game up until I learned through trial and painful error that women loathe a man who needs to be instructed on how to actually be more attractive to women. I didn't understand that by my subscribing to this spoon-fed feminization Game and overtly advocating for it I was only advertising to the very girls I wanted that I *Just Didn't Get It.*

This was simply the first stage of Game changing for me, and I'm fairly certain that you'd read a similar story from most of the manosphere's heaviest hitters. I'm peripherally familiar with the early histories of the likes of blogger/PUAs like Roosh, Nick Krauser and even Mystery, so I don't think it's too much of a stretch to say that the Game they practice today would be foreign to their younger selves.

When I moved into my rock star 20's I began practicing a new form of Game, one based on social proof and demonstrating higher value (DHV).

Of course I had no idea I was practicing any Game at the time. I had reinvented myself and my identity shifted into that of a guy who was Spinning Plates, being more self-concerned and enjoying the benefits of that social proof and DHV; but if you'd asked me what I'd done to effect that change, or how my Game was affected by it, I wouldn't have been able to give you an answer then – Game was just instinctual for me.

Now in my married years, as a husband and the father of a teenage daughter, and my professional life in the liquor and casino world where I interact with beautiful women on a weekly basis, I still employ Game when I don't realize I am.

However, that Game is the compounded, internalized result of what I've learned and used since the days I believed in the "be nice for girls to like you" teenage Game. Amused Mastery, Command Presence and a few other principles became much easier to employ as a mature man, but also a new grasp of how women's lives have a more or less predictable pattern to them.

Thanks to my time studying behavioral psychology I understand the methods women use to prompt and provoke men (shit tests). Thanks to my Red Pill awareness and simple understand of how women's biology influences hypergamy I now understand why they do so – and more importantly, how to avoid the traps of falling into the worst aspects of women's dualistic sexual strategy.

All of this influences my 'Game' in the now. As before, I don't play a constant, conscious game of mental chess in my dealings with women (and even the men in my social and professional life), I just live it.

It's important to consider that the concept of Game you might be struggling with now was probably some other man's experience before you encountered it. What is Game for me at 46, will most likely not have the exact same utility for me at 56, but if I stay sharp and learn along the way I'll develop a new Game for that phase of life.

In Roosh's book, *Poosy Paradise*, he has a quote in it that struck me (I paraphrase):

> *There are a lot of men who tell me they wish they knew back then what they know now, but in all likelihood that knowledge wouldn't serve them as well as they believe it would. They'd simply make new mistakes (and hopefully learn from them) based on the things they never had any experience of in the now.*

There is always additional knowledge a man can know even when he possess the highest level of knowledge.

THE MALE EXPERIENCE

A little over sixteen years ago my wife was pregnant with our daughter. For most of her adult life Mrs. Tomassi has been a medical professional (medical imaging) so while she was pregnant she and her girl-friends at the hospital would take any free moment they got to sneak into the ultrasound room a have a peek at our gestating daughter. As a result we have about 4 times as many ultrasound pictures as most other couples get. I actually have images of my daughter as a multi-celled organism.

It was during one of these impromptu scannings that we discovered what gender our child would be. We were both more than a bit impatient and didn't want to wait for the silly build up the OBGYN would make of revealing her gender, so we hit up a girl-friend of my wife to do another ultrasound around the right trimester.

She scanned for a bit and said, "Oh yeah, you've got a girl." We asked how she could be so sure and she said, "Her hands aren't in the right place." Then she explained, "Almost always when the baby is a boy his hands will be down around his crotch once he's matured to a certain phase in the pregnancy. There's not much else to do in there, so they play with themselves. Your daughter's hands are usually up around her face."

After hearing this I began to appreciate the power of testosterone. Whenever I read someone tell me sex isn't really a "need", I think about how even in the womb the influence of testosterone is there. For better or worse, our lives as Men center on our capacity to control, unleash, mitigate and direct that influence.

Socially we build up appropriate conventions intended to bind it into some kind of uniformity, to prevent the destructive potential and exploit its constructive potential – while personally we develop convictions, psychologies and internalized rules by order of degree to live our lives with its influence always running in the background of our subconsciousness.

Experience

Women become very indignant when trying to understand the male experience.

This is due in most part to women's innate solipsism and their presumption that their experience is the universal one. Part of this presumption is due to social reinforcement, but that social presumption – essentially the equalist presumption – is rooted in women's base indifference to anything external that doesn't affect them directly and personally. If everyone is essentially the same and equal, and we're acculturated to encourage this perspective, it leaves women to interpret their own imperatives and innate solipsism to be the normative ones for men.

So it often comes with a lot shock and indignation (which women instinctively crave) when women are forced, sometimes rudely, to acknowledge that men's experience doesn't reflect their own.

The reactive response is to force-fit men's experience into women's self-concerned interpretations of what that experience *should* be according to a feminine-primary perception of what works best for women. On an individual woman's level this amounts to denial and rejection of a legitimate male-primary experience through shame or implied fem-centric obligations to accept and adopt her experience as his responsibility. On a social level this conflict is reflected in social conventions and feminine-centric social doctrines, as well as being written directly into binding laws that forcibly enact a feminine-centric perspective into our social fabric.

Feminine solipsism and the primacy of the female experience superseding the male experience begins with the individual woman (micro) and extrapolates into a feminine primary social construct (macro).

Virtually every conflict between the sexes comes back to the rejection of the legitimacy of the male experience.

In every social and psychological dynamic I've ever written about it's the fundamental lack of understanding of the male experience which influences women's perception of our sex. Whether it's understanding our sexual impulse, our idealistic concept of love, or appreciating the sacrifices men uniquely make to facilitate a feminine reality, the disconnect always distills down to a fundamental lack of accepting the legitimacy of the male experience.

It would be too easy a cop out to simply write this disconnect off as an existential difference. Obviously men and women cannot spend time in each other's skin to directly appreciate the experience of the other. However, since the Feminine Imperative is the normative one in our current social makeup the presumption is that a feminine directed 'equalism' is the *only* legitimate experience. Thus the masculine experience is, by default, delegitimized, if not vilified, for simply reminding the feminine that inherent, evolved sexual differences challenge equalism by masculinity's very presence.

I reject your reality and replace it with my own...

Men just *being* men is a passive challenge to the Feminine Imperative; Red Pill awareness is a direct challenge to the legitimacy of a feminine primary experience. It's important to recall here that the primacy of the female experience begins on the personal level with an individual woman and then exponentially multiplies into a social (macro) scale. When you assert yourself as a Red Pill Man, you are asserting your disconnection from that feminine-primary frame. This begins on a personal level for a woman, and then extrapolates into a social affront for all women.

The initial shock (and indignation) is one of interrupting her comfortable, predictable expectations of men in the feminine defined reality she experiences for herself. As even the most rookie of Red Pill Men will attest, the legitimate female experience rejects this assertion, most times with an amount of hostility.

Men are met with socially reinforced, prepared responses designed to defend against attempts to question the legitimacy of the feminine experience as the primary one – shaming is often the first recourse, even most passive challenges warrant shaming, but character assassination and disqualifications based upon a feminine primary perspective are the go-to weapons of the solipsistic nature of the feminine mindset (even when men are the ones subscribing to it).

The next weapon in the feminine psychological arsenal is histrionics.

Aggrandized exaggerations and overblown straw man tactics may seem like a last resort for women to a man attempting to rationally impose his Red Pill, legitimized, male experience, but know histrionics for what they are – a carefully design, feminine-specific and socially approved failsafe for women.

In the same vein as a Woman's Prerogative (women reserve the rightness of changing their minds) and the Feminine Mystique, female histrionics are a legitimized and socially excusable tactic with the latent purpose of protecting a woman's solipsistic experience. She's an emotional creature and your challenge to her ego only brings out the hysteric in her – it's men's fault that they *don't get it*, and it's men's fault for bringing it out in her by challenging her solipsism. And thus is she excused from her protective histrionics at men's cost.

It's important for Red Pill Men to understand what their presence, much less their assertions, mean to the feminine; their very existence, just their questioning, represents a challenge to individual, ego-invested feminine solipsism.

Always be prepared for the inevitable defense of a woman's self-importance. Even in the most measured approach, you are essentially breaking a woman's self-concept by reminding or asserting that her experience is not the universal experience. There's a temptation for Red Pill Men to get comfortable with a woman's who accepts Red Pill truths, only to find that her ego will just accept the parts of those truths that its comfortable with and benefits from. That solipsism doesn't die once she's acknowledged the legitimacy of your experience, anymore than your sexual imperative dies if you accept her experience as the legitimate one.

The Love Experience

How then can men and women love each other intensely and genuinely in an era of unapologetic feminine primacy and unignorable open Hypergamy? After absorbing the import of the time line of women's maturity and the prime directive it demands from men in a feminine-primary social order, you'll probably be left with some hesitancy to believe that a shared love can ever be possible in a complementary sense.

The first thing we need to consider is the male experience vs. the female experience. I hate to get too existential, but it comes down to our individuated experiences as men and women. I'm going to give two examples here.

There's an interesting conflict of societal messaging we get from an equalitarian / feminine-primary social order. This is one that simultaneously tells us that "we are not so different" or "we are more alike than we are different" and then, yet implores us to still "celebrate our diversity" and "embrace (or tolerate) our differences" as people.

This is easily observable in issues of multiculturalism, but it also universally crosses over into issues of gender. The most popular equalist trope is that concepts of gender are only social constructs and that women and men are comparative, existential equals and only their physical plumbing makes them different in form.

From a Red Pill perspective we see the error in evidence of this egalitarian fantasy. I've written countless posts and essays on the evidential and logical fallacies that make up gender equalism, but the important thing to be aware of is the conflict inherent within that belief – equalism expects men and women's *existential* experiences to be the same, while at the same time pleads that we embrace the differences it purports we don't actually have.

It fundamentally denies the separation, from an evolved biological / psychological perspective, that men and women experience life in different ways. The idea is that it's the nebulous *'society'* that fiendishly determines our gender experiences and less, if nothing, of it is truly influenced by a human being's psychological-biological firmware.

I had a commenter drop the following in one of my related threads:

> *I think men have no innate desire to marry up. Hypergamy doesn't compute for us. I know what hunger feels like and I assume women feel it the same way I do. I'm empathetic to poor, hungry children because I know what they're feeling. However I have no idea what hypergamy feels like. I've never felt it's pull.*

My second example comes from the *Women & Sex* section in *The Rational Male* in which I explore the fallacy of the social convention that insists "women are just as sexual as men" and that "women want sex, enjoy sex, even more than men."

This canard is both observably and biologically disprovable, but the presumption is based on the same "we're all the same, but celebrate the difference" conflicting principle that I mentioned above. If a dynamic is complimentary to the feminine then the biological basis is one we're expected to 'embrace the diversity' of, but if the dynamic is unflattering to the feminine it's the result "of a society that's fixated on teaching gender roles to ensure the Patriarchy, we're really more alike than not."

The idea is patently false because there is no real way any woman can experience the existence and conditions that a man does throughout his life. I mention in that essay about how a female amateur body builder I knew who was dumbstruck by how horny she became after her first cycle of anabolic steroids. "I can't believe men can live in a state like this" were her exact words. She was just beginning to get a taste of what men experience and control in their own skins 24-hours a day and it was unsettling for her.

Women are used to a cyclic experience of sexuality, whereas men must be ready to perform at the first, best opportunity sexually. These are our individuated experiences and despite all the bleating of the equalists they are qualitatively different. No man has any idea of what Hypergamy feels like. To my knowledge there is no drug or hormone that can simulate the existential experience of Hypergamy. Even if there were, men and women's minds are fundamentally wired differently, so the simulated experience could never be replicated for a man.

I understand how Hypergamy works from observing the behavior and understanding the motivating biology for it. I also understand that our species evolved with, and benefited from it – or at least it makes deductive sense that what we know as Hypergamy today is a derivative of that evolution – but what I don't have is a firsthand, existential experience of Hypergamy and I never will. Likewise, women will never have a similar existential experience of what it's like to be a man.

So it should be an easy follow to deduce that how a woman experiences love, as based on her Hypergamic opportunistic impulses, is a fundamentally different experience than that of a man's. The equalist social order wants love to be an equal, mutual, agreement on a definition of love that transcends individuated gender experience, but it simply will not accept that an intersexual experience of love is defined by each sex's individuated experience.

I have no doubt that there are areas of crossover in both men's idealistic concept of love and women's opportunistic concept, but this experience of love is still defined by gender-specific individuation. By that I mean that women can and do experience intense feelings of love for a man based on her Hypergamously influenced criteria for love.

If you sift through the comments of forums regarding women's 'love experience you'll come across examples of women describing in great detail how deeply they love their husbands / boyfriends, and are in complete disarray over being told their love stems from Hypergamic opportunism.

I have no doubt that their feelings of love are genuine to them based on their individuated concepts of love; indeed they're ready to fight you tooth and nail to defend their investment in those feelings. What I'm saying is that the criteria a man should need to meet in order to generate those emotions and arrive at a love state are not the universally mutual criteria which an equalitarian social order would have the whole of society believe.

So, yes, men and women can and do love each other intensely and genuinely – *from their own individuated experiences.* The processes they used to come to this love state differs in concept and existential individuation, and what sustains that love state is still dependent upon the criteria of men's idealistic, and women opportunistic concepts of love.

The Cardinal Rule of Sexual Strategies:
For one gender's sexual strategy to succeed the other gender must compromise or abandon their own.

The commodification of that love state is presently weighted on the feminine because the Feminine Imperative is socially ascendant. The importance of satisfying the female sexual (and really life-goal) strategy takes primary social precedence today. Thus men's individuated experience is devalued to an assumption of an "it's-all-equal" universality while women's is blown up out of all real valuation with collective expectations of "embracing their unique difference" set apart from that universality. If men's experience is one-size-fits-all it's really a small, and socially blameless, step for a woman to withhold the reward criteria men place on their idealistic love in order to satisfy their own sexual strategy.

Women's social primacy allows them to feel good about themselves for commodifying the idealistic rewards men value to come to their own state of love, as well as maintain it.

It is one further step to embrace the concept that men's experience of love, the idealism he applies to it and even his own sexual and life imperatives are in fact the same as those of women's – while still setting women's apart when it serves them better. Thus the cardinal rule of sexual strategies comes to a feminine-primary consolidation by socially convincing men that women's experience and imperatives are, or should be considered to be, the same as men's individuated experiences. Add women's already innate solipsism to this and you have a formula for a gender-universal presumption of the experience of love based primarily on the individuated female experience of love.

In other words, women expect men to socially and psychologically agree with, reinforce and cooperate with the opportunistic feminine model of love as the equalist, gender-mutual model of love while still believing that women share their own idealistic model. It's the *correct* model that should work for everyone, or so women's solipsism would have us believe.

MIDLIFE EPIPHANIES

It's ironic that a man should be made to feel infantile, or "less than responsible" for indulging in his own wants. For certain, a surprise sports car purchase may be an extreme example, but sometimes over-exaggeration is necessary to illustrate a larger point. That larger point is the nature in which women in a feminine-primary social order exercises de facto personal and social control over men. It's part of the feminine Matrix to think that 'responsibility' should be uniquely framed in what best serves the feminine. Due to a lifetime of conditioning we literally don't know any other way to interpret it most of the time.

When a man begins to 'go rogue' the Feminine Imperative has many pre-established social conventions to mediate this. Obviously designating men's correct role as 'responsibility' to serve the feminine frame is the social control, but there are other powerful conventions that the imperative uses. One of these is the Myth of the Midlife Crisis.

A lot of hokey comedies have been produced covering midlife crises. Usually the main characters are cast as overweight schlubs trying to recapture their by-gone days. In real life men are ridiculed, usually around age 40, for losing their mojo and acting 'irresponsibly' or 'erratically' in some silly gesture of reclaiming his independence. However, this masculine shaming hides a more desperate latent purpose for the feminine.

The SMV Crossover

The most stereotypical midlife crisis occurs for a man around age 40. As I illustrate in the SMV graph it's important to remember that a man's sexual market value really begins to peak between 36-38. It's usually at this point that the most Blue Pill of men begin to see the design in women's sexual strategy, the role he now realizes he's committed himself to, and have the best chance to truly unplug from the Matrix.

It is also at this point that the threat of a man becoming self-aware of his now fully developed SMV has its greatest urgency for women to repress him from realizing. Even life-long Blue Pill men generally come to an understanding that their wives' SMV has dropped and realize their own SMV is comparatively greater. For the first time in his relationship history, he faces the Cardinal Rule of Relationships from his own perspective – women need him more than he needs women.

The Feminine Imperative has come to expect this awakening. In decades past, before there was a formalized Game, before there was the connectivity we have today, the Feminine Imperative relied upon social controls that limited a man's becoming aware of his SMV. Through pop-culture and mass media men were taught to expect a prefabricated personal 'crisis', even enlisting men to promote the idea themselves.

However, the imperative casts the 'crisis' as irresponsible and juvenile. It relied upon the time-tested shaming of masculinity in the hope men would self-regulate when the time came that his SMV outclassed that of the woman in his life. So we got hokey movies, and the presumptuous ridicule of men wanting to trade-up their wives for 'trophy wives'; because even when a man is mature and established he must be made to believe he'll still be little better than a cad if he's given some marginal success in life.

Midlife Awareness

Probably the most common story I experienced when I did peer counseling was the disillusioned married guy.

Most of these guys were professionals, mid to late 30's and all their stories were the same:

> *"I feel like I've done everything anyone ever expected of me for the past 10-15 years and I get no appreciation for it."*

These guys "did the right thing" and either their wives' were unresponsive to them or they still viewed these men as a "fixer upper" project that they'd been perpetually working on over a 20 year marriage.

This experience is what helped me to better understand the Myth of the Midlife Crisis. Men, in most western culture's do in fact experience a midlife crisis, but this isn't due to the trivialized and oft ridiculed pop culture reasoning.

Women, and feminization, would have us believe that men experiencing a midlife crisis need to buy a sports car or divorce their wives in favor of a 'trophy wife' due to some repressed need to recapture their lost youth.

This of course fits into the feminized myth that men are egoisitic, simple creatures and masculinity is infantile in nature, but this only serves to reassure women that they "still got it" at 40.

The truth about men's midlife crises isn't about recapturing youth, it's about finally understanding the trappings they've been sold into through their 20's and 30's and coming to terms with that often horrible truth. They are forced to confront the part they've inadvertently played in facilitating a woman's sexual strategy that was sold to him as his feminine-correct social responsibility.

They come to the point on the time line when a woman's maturity phase places her in the more necessitous position that he's been in for the better part of his 20s and likely half of his 30s. He's emotionally invested in her, or if not, the idealism of how he was sold a 'healthy relationship' should be, and this conflicts with both his realizing his SMV (or his lost potential of it) and confronting the reality of the part he played in facilitating her duplicitous sexual strategy.

Some men do in fact buy the sports car, get the new hotty wife or act in some fashion that appears reckless and irresponsible. This isn't due to infantilism, but rather a new understanding of their own position as men. They've "lived responsibly" for so long and for so little appreciation that when that true realization is made they feel the need to move. The true nature of the Game that's been perpetrated on them becomes clear and they need to react.

They've become respected, put in the hours, the sacrifice, the censoring of their own views, priorities and imperatives. They realize now that they've sold off true passions in favor of maintaining what others have told him was his responsibility – whether it was his choice or not.

And all for what? A fat wife? A shrew? Maybe even a fantastic marriage and a wonderful family life, but also a nagging doubt about not seeing enough of the world or accomplishing what *he* wanted to do by 40 because of it – a nagging doubt that he's not living up to his curse of potential.

In truth, I worry about men who don't come to this crisis, these are the men who are truly lost. These are the guys who remain life long Blue Pills, happy in their ignorance or forcing down truths too terrible to acknowledge.

THE MATURE MAN

I once got into an interesting debate about the reasons why mature men tend to opt for younger women with whom to settle down with. As is to be expected from fem-screech and their male enablers the social shaming mechanisms abounded. Most of these are some variation of the "men's fragile egos" canard or the "a real man would want to get with a woman his own age" trope. This quote pretty much summed up the opposing point:

> *"Older guys want to bang college-age girls for the same reason that many older women like dating younger guys: to live in a state of suspended youth and be reminded that they 'still got it'".*

I half-agree. Older women definitely want to think they "still got it", with regards to their capacity to hold the attention of younger guys they find themselves in competition with younger women for.

However, older men who naturally pursue younger women come to realize that they've "finally got it". Why wouldn't a guy of 40 have a natural preference for the younger woman after reaching a level of maturity and accomplishment that allows him this? Professional women tied to the male template of life's progression tend to think that they too should be entitled to the sexual attraction of 'eligible' men by virtue of their mature achievements, professional status, education and some imagined sense of knowing themselves better.

They are mistaken.

The Associations of Maturity

First off, it's a mistake to just peg 40 year old men in this demographic. There are plenty of early to mid thirties guys who can and do pull girls 5 to 8 years younger than themselves with some regularity. Funny how there's little shaming stigma with that age difference.

It's not a man's physical age so much as what that age popularly represents (or is perceived to represent) – maturity, accomplishment, better provisioning capacity, status, education, etc. and all the trappings a man who's realized the best of his potential should have attained.

Do *all* men actually realize these to their satisfaction by this time?

Of course not, but it's the perception that they *should* have actualized this that is the attractant in comparison to younger guys who haven't, nor could they really be expected to. Mature Men represent this perception of assumed accomplishment and security – exactly what women are looking for in a phase of life where their sexual marketability declines and their need for long term provisioning becomes more urgent.

Second, understand that the incidence of 30-40 year old men remaining single up to this time of life is rare. Most guys (Betas in majority) are already engaged by 26 years old and/or have been serial monogamists up to this point.

For all the recent hand wringing about 'kidult' men not manning up and marrying post-Epiphany Phase women, rare is the guy who remains single into his late 30s. By the time he arrives at his SMV peak period he's either divorced once or on marriage number two.

Still fewer come into the realization of their own vastly increased sexual market value assuming they've managed to stay in shape and accomplish things financially, emotionally and maturity-wise up to this point and *then* use this to their own advantage with younger women. An interesting aside here is that men are berated for being peter-pans in their late 20s for not living up to female entitlement, then get the same treatment for marrying younger women when they do mature into Men. This is a glaring illustration of the female imperative at work.

Now add to that a constant feminine social convention convincing them they have "fragile egos" or shames them for dating young 'chippys' (i.e. future trophy wives) instead of mature women (generally single mothers) with all their accompanying baggage.

Unsurprisingly we see in most cultures older males striving for the attentions of the younger and more attractive females, but in western culture he becomes vilified and shamed for this – or at least that's what western-feminized women would like to be the case.

The most common complaint women in their mid-thirties bemoan is that, "There's no good men" or they can't understand why men just can't "grow up".

Increasingly 'career women' desiring to finally start a family at age 35 find that men – particularly the ones that meet their equalist provisioning criteria – in their age range (33-38) are not interested in women (to say nothing of 'career women') of their age. They're interested in the 22 year olds who wouldn't give them the time of day when they didn't have the status (or maturity) that they've just discovered they now have.

And of course the 35 year old careerist woman was one of these 22 year old girls, only 13 years prior, who was doing precisely the same thing the 22 year old girls are doing in their Party Years today.

Midlife Epiphany

These Men are not trying to "relive" anything; generally they never "lived" the experiences which they're accused of trying to recreate.

However, they are newly aware of their own sexual market value – and nothing both frightens and attracts a woman so well as a Man aware of his own sexual market value to women. That's the foundation of midlife confidence, and, if he's capitalized on his potential to some degree, this gives him a mature gravitas that attracts women.

This represents a problem for women though. They want a Man with the confidence and maturity (derived from experience) to make important decisions, be an initiator, a good provider, etc., but not *so* confident that he weighs his options and selects her *out* of his provisioning for a competing woman based on his primary requisite of physical arousal and sexual availability.

To counter this, the feminine creates social conventions that shame a Man for considering a woman too much younger than herself. This has the latent intent of leveling the SMP playing field in order for her to compete with women who are younger, hotter and more sexually available than a woman progressed in years.

He has to be kept ignorant of the whole process, but still shamed enough into thinking his desire for the young and attractive mid 20s girl makes him "juvenile" or preoccupied with a "fragile ego", or "trying to recapture his youth". The feminine reality demands he be dissuaded from pursuing his interests in favor of women's sexual strategies, and the best way to do that is to slime his interests as a perversion.

"To most college-age girls, a guy in his 40s (even 30s) and up is usually the 'creepy old man' even if he takes good care of himself. The old guy usually ends up trying to fit into the young girl's world instead of the other way around."

This common refrain of the Feminine Imperative is the Creepy Old Man tactic. I don't necessarily disagree with this as an observation, however I believe its effect is contextual.

I'm regularly at events (mixers, clubs, promos, trade shows, etc.) as part of my work where I'm approached by much younger women. If the 40 year old guy is perceived to be attempting to "fit in" with that age's social peers, then this is absolutely correct.

The disconnect comes from a man who'd otherwise be perceived as possessing the attributes he should have for his age trying to retrofit himself into another generation's social profile. That is when he becomes the "old guy in the club".

Never attempt to 'backdate' yourself style-wise, linguistically, etc. If you're attractive, the girls who want to associate with a mature Man will find *you*.

Complaints

Men become happier than women by mid-life and for the most part I think I can see why. Most women in their late 30s to mid 40s are, for the most part, chronic complainers.

After going through the high drama phases of her 20s, into kids, marriages and divorces in her 30s, women tend to content themselves languishing in this dissatisfaction that her fantasy life isn't panning out to be. Nothing measures up to the perceived ideals she thinks are her due.

Most women in western culture who find themselves single at 38-42 are there after an earlier life that didn't go as planned. They almost universally carry some kind of baggage.

Can they be attractive? Uncommonly, but yes. However it's a mistake to presume older (or at least age level peers) women to be more intellectually equitable with older men and therefore more compatible choices for LTRs or marriage.

I'm sorry if this comes off as glossing myself, but honestly, I've encountered very few women I can relate to intellectually or that I'd consider equal in my particular interests, my life experiences, my passions, etc. or share the same degree of experiential curiosity. That's not a cut on the whole of women, just an illustration of the difference in the genders' maturation.

I wish this didn't sound like conceit on my part because, in all humility, I think the better part of what I find important is really pretty mundane. It's not that I hold a low opinion of women's capacity to be more 'life-curious'; it's simply their own general indifference to even trying to relate to that in comparison to their own distractions.

I don't think women (and particularly 35-40 year old women) feel it's incumbent upon them to *have* to be a good mate, intellectually stimulating, a good mother, or even a good sexual partner for a Man's consideration. I'd attribute most of that to the female sense of entitlement and victimhood that permeates feminine popular culture, but also to men and women's interests really being fundamentally disparate. In other words, with the extraordinarily rare exception, women will *rarely* put forth the same effort a man will for a woman to better identify herself with his interests for the explicit purpose of being a better mate for him. That burden of performance uniquely belongs to men.

"Mature" Women

Obviously a more mature woman will have a greater urgency to settle into the long term provisioning security that marriage provides her, but this urgency gets confused with actual maturity. Just because a woman is more motivated to start a family and enter into a more traditionally domestic life doesn't mean she's an intellectual or mature equal – nor does it make her more compatible with you in this sense just by virtue of her progressed phase of maturity. It simply means she is more motivated to do so based on her conditions of diminishing sexual value.

I think on some level of consciousness, older, more mature men who've spent a good portion of their lives dealing with the experiences that create this life baggage older women accrue, recognize a necessity to distance themselves from it.

After making the sacrifices, and avoiding (or not) the pitfalls that he must to become the healthy, mature and accomplished man that older women complain are in such short supply, I think it's pretty matter-of-fact to seek out a younger, hotter, more sexually available woman with little to no baggage. The counter to this is the feminine social conventions of shame that I covered earlier.

Men on a basic functioning level are pragmatists, even when we do allow our emotions to get the better of us. One tenet we maintain is an understanding that women tend to operate from an emotional level, whereas men tend to operate from deductive reasoning.

While a hot piece of ass is it's own motivation, I think on some level, after the necessary experiences, sacrifices and time it takes to get to a point of personal maturity, we see a younger woman with less baggage as a sort of double bonus.

If I were to find myself single tomorrow, this would be exactly my motivation.

Why would I invest my considerable capacity for financial, emotional, intellectual and security provisioning into complicating my own life with a woman fraught with the baggage of her own failings and inconsistencies of the last 15-20 years?

For what I've become myself and what I know is valuable, why would I not look for a simplification considering what was required of me to get to that maturity? If middle age men are happier than women at this stage of life, it's because they've arrived at a place where they don't feel the need to qualify themselves to women any longer – and realize the reverse is now true.

A rich man doesn't need to tell you he's rich. You can see it in his appearance, his mannerisms, his bearing. The same is true for a mature Man. In his maturity he's comfortable in the knowledge that he doesn't need to prove it by qualifying himself to social conventions that are counter to his own self-interest and his well being.

CHAPTER 9

A NEW HOPE

Worst part of the Red Pill?

Seeing how I fucked it all up. Really.

There's days when I get up in the morning, sit on the edge of the bed, and just feel like I wish I could forget what I've learned. I wish I could close Pandora's Box and stuff all the knowledge of the stupid shit I've done back in there. Just go back to sleep and plug back in.

But then I realize: while I can see how fucked up things are and that's a bit depressing, I was completely and utterly fucking miserable when I didn't know all that I've learned. Like when the Blue Pill was all I knew, my misery was worse because I didn't realize where my power to change things ended and the things I couldn't change began. It left me with a feeling of so little power and control that I was miserable.

There's a lot of research that says a big part of "happiness" in a person's life is a feeling of agency. I felt none. I was fumbling in the dark.

Now I can see where I fucked up, and there's a lot of mistakes I made that were choices under my control. But I didn't know it at the time if I'm being honest. Young, stupid, ignorant me just didn't know. But I also, each day, see more and more clearly what is and is not in my control.

Further, before I wouldn't have known how to control the things that I could control even if I had known what they were. Now I learn more each day about controlling them.

Ignorance might be bliss in some respects (especially when looking back on your own life), but when ignorance was the cause of your misery it pays to remember why you educated yourself. Remember why you took those steps. While you're looking back at how you fucked up, think long and hard about why you fucked up. There's a good chance you didn't understand things well enough to make a good choice. That's where my trying to be fair with myself about past mistakes comes from.

Try really hard to remember what it was like being 'young you'.

Why did you make those choices? Did you understand risk/reward properly? Did you have a Socratic understanding of your own ignorance?

Did you have enough experience to know for a fact that something was a bad choice? Were you aware enough of your own biology working against you to counteract its bad decisions?

I bet you were a lot more ignorant and inexperienced than a cursory glance at old mistakes from your current point in life lets you realize. I know I was.

— Sun Wukong, comment on The Rational Male

CHAPTER 10

NEW HOPE

In the first book, towards the end of *The Bitter Taste of the Red Pill* I wrote this:

> *The truth will set you free, but it doesn't make truth hurt any less, nor does it make truth any prettier, and it certainly doesn't absolve you of the responsibilities that truth requires. One of the biggest obstacles guys face in unplugging is accepting the hard truths that Game forces upon them. Among these is bearing the burden of realizing what you've been conditioned to believe for so long were comfortable ideals and loving expectations are really liabilities. Call them lies if you want, but there's a certain hopeless nihilism that accompanies categorizing what really amounts to a system that you are now cut away from. It is not that you're hopeless, it's that you lack the insight at this point to see that you can create hope in a new system – one in which you have more direct control over.*

One of the hardest lessons I had to learn when I unplugged was throwing away 'hope'.

Not real, internal, personal hope, but rather the '*hope*' I had been led to believe was a realizable state – if circumstances, if personalities, if fate or some other condition defined by the feminine imperative would just align in such a way that I'd been conditioned to believe it could, then that feminine defined contentment could be actualized.

I wanted very much to realize that idealized state by defining hope (or having it defined for me) in a context that was never of my own real choosing. I got just as depressed as anyone else when I unplugged. I got angry. I didn't want to think that I'd invested so much of myself in something that was fundamentally unattainable because my understanding of it had been incorrect, either by purpose or by my own hopeful interpretations of it. Turns out it was both.

My own 'unplugging' was a gradual affair and came after a lot of drawn out trauma. And yes, to realize that all of that trauma amounted to nothing after hoping and struggling to mold myself into something that I was led to believe was achievable was even more depressing.

It wasn't until I realized that the hope I was sold on came from the same social paradigm that never held my best interests as a priority that I threw it away. That was a tough day because I realized in doing so I would have to find a new sense of hope for myself. It seemed very nihilistic at the time, and I had to really make a determined effort not to make that choice from a sense of self-pity.

One particularly hard revelation I had to disabuse myself of was understanding that women's concept of love differs from that of men. That was tough to embrace because the old hope I was struggling to realize was based on the primary tenet of Blue Pill thinking; the equalist notion that men and women share a mutually acknowledged, mutually accepted, concept of love.

Once I understood this was an idealization rather than a reality, and that women can and do love men deeply, but in an entirely different female-specific opportunistic concept of love, I discovered that I no longer 'hoped' for that mutuality. It was then I embraced the hope that men and women could still genuinely love each other from their own perspectives of love without needing a mutual consensus.

I remembered then an older man I had done some peer counseling with while in college and how this man had essentially striven his entire life to please and content his ex-wife, and his now second wife of more than 30 years. From his early 20s he'd spent his personal life in the hopeful attempt at contenting, appeasing and qualifying for a mutually shared state of love which he believed these women (the only 2 he'd ever had sex with) had a real capacity for.

At 73 (now) he's spent his life invested in a hope that simply doesn't exist – that he can be loved as a man ideally believes a woman ought to be able to love him – just as all the romantic, feminine-defined ideals of love he'd learned from a feminine-centric social order had convinced him of for so long.

This is why I say men are the True Romantics, because the overwhelming majority will devote a lifetime to the effort of actualizing a belief in a male-idealized love to find fulfillment in a woman and for that woman. Men will dedicate, and take their own lives to realize this.

Old Hope for New Hope

I hope all that doesn't sound too fortune cookie for you, but it's a prime example of redefining hope in a new Red Pill-aware paradigm. You can hope and thrive in a new Red Pill context – I know I have – but it's much easier when you internalize Red Pill truths and live with them in a Red Pill context instead of force-fitting them into your old, feminine-defined, Blue Pill context. I can imagine what my marriage would look like if I hadn't made the Red Pill transition and learned to use that awareness in it. There are a lot of guys paying 'marriage coaches' $150 an hour because they never did.

There was a great comment I received in this regard that was too good not to include in its entirety here:

I think I get it!

For years I have been bitter about this need to "perform" about how this shows that women do not love us as we love etc.. And just now I was reviewing my old relationships and I recalled something.

In each of my relationships, prior to meeting the women I eventually fell in love with, I was constantly working on myself, I would get in shape, hang out with friends, explore my environment and work on myself and my music etc. As soon as I would "fall in love" I would slowly drop those activities, I'd focus on being a good bf, I would focus on providing and "being what she wanted" what I thought she wanted, better said.

But here is my Eureka moment, what I recalled each time was being unhappy, what I recall each time was feeling boxed in and kind of dull...of feeling trapped.

Is this what Rollo means when he says our response to women is a conditioning, and that the sadness we get from Red Pill truth is the result of behaving and believing something that is not really our nature, but the result of having someone else's behaviors and beliefs installed into us?

So I think I finally understand it for myself... the talk of putting yourself first, of "performing" etc is really just a way of saying "you don't have to do what people say you're supposed to do in a relationship – you don't have to drop everything for her, you don't have to stop doing what you like and love and you don't have to kiss her ass"

In my case I dropped everything for two reasons. One was to do what I thought I was supposed to do...what I heard women say they wanted from a man, what my mother said a man should be etc., and the second reason was insecurity. I wanted her to love me, I didn't want to rock the boat, I was scared of losing her...so eventually I did. I believed that in order for me to be worthy of her, of her love, I had to go along and give her what she said she wanted, what I was taught she wanted.

Is this what Rollo and everyone else is talking about? Because I think I finally get it.

Up to now I have faked my Game, to some extent. I just knew better than to do certain things or did things I knew would make me attractive, etc. to women. But seeing this now, not only am I realizing there is nothing to be bitter about – I was always happier working on myself and my interests and actually resentful of having to stop them – but that I am actually happier doing this thing women want of us we call "performing".

In a way, you are performing, as Rollo says, either way. If you stop and think you can rest, in many ways you are doing so because you have been conditioned to believe, as I was, that you should. That real love meant you could and should.

Anyway, maybe this is simply me and my personal experience of it, but it makes sense to me.. and I think this has revealed to me something monumental, personally. Maybe other guys have a different experience of it, but this is how I have seen it played out in my life.

I feel better.

Unlearning

The key to living in a Red Pill context is to unlearn your Blue Pill expectations and dreams of finding contentment in them and replace them with expectations and aspirations based on realistic understandings of Red Pill truths.

Learn this now, you will never achieve contentment or emotional fulfillment in a Blue Pill context with Red Pill awareness.

Killing your inner Beta is a difficult task and part of that is discarding an old, comfortable, Blue Pill paradigm. For many newly unplugged, Red Pill aware, men the temptation is to think they can use this new understanding to achieve the goal-states of their preconditioned Blue Pill ideals. What they don't understand is that, not only are those Blue Pill goal-states flawed, but they are also based on a flawed understanding of how to attain them.

Red Pill awareness demands a Red Pill context for fulfillment. Never seek emotional fulfillment through women. Blue Pill fulfillment is based on feminine-primary, Blue Pill conditions for that contentment. Even when men achieve these Blue Pill goal-states, the ones they're conditioned to believe they should want for themselves, they find themselves discontent with those states and trapped by the liabilities of them.

The periods when a man is not striving to achieve or maintain those Blue Pill goal-states are the times he will be most fulfilled with his life, talents and ambitions.

As if this weren't enough to convince a man he needs to re-imagine himself in a Red Pill-primary context, when women are presented with 'the perfect guy' in a Blue Pill context they gradually (sometimes immediately) come to despise him. As proven by their actions, even women don't want that Blue Pill perfected goal-state because it stagnates the otherwise exciting, self-important men they are aroused by, and attracted to, in a Red Pill context.

"Women should only ever be a complement to a man's life, never the focus of it."

Living in a Blue Pill context, and hoping you can achieve fulfillment in its fundamentally flawed goal-states, conditions men to make women the focus of their lives.

Throw that hope away and understand that you can create hope in a new system – one in which you have more direct control over.

AFTERWORD

"So what's the endgame Rollo?"

"By subscribing to your Preventative Medicine plan, men can and will protect themselves from being casualties of the Feminine Imperative. But what are we ultimately striving for? Is it to remain in a perpetual state of plate-spinning bliss? Do we game the older hens and then leave them clucking when they make their stake for commitment? Do we just ignore women unless they're under 27 and down to fuck?"

As I mentioned in the introduction, this series probably wont address particular personal issues some readers will want it to. I also understand that while I can provide this outline, it doesn't really go into depth about *how* a man might use this knowledge to his best advantage with *his* particular woman. However, my hope is that it will put certain behaviors and mindsets you find in a woman, and how they align or don't align with this outline, into something more understandable for your individual experience. This is in no way comprehensive or meant to account for every woman's circumstance, but rather to help a man with what he can expect in various phases.

It's preventive medicine, not a cure for any particular disease.

Imagine for a moment I had the temerity to presume that I know exactly what a 60 year old reader experiences in his personal life with a post-menopausal wife. I could take a good stab at it (in fact I have an essay about dealing with menopause) but anything specific I could prescribe for him would be based on my best-guess speculations and according to how I've observed and detailed issues in this series or any of my past work.

From my earliest posts on the SoSuave forum I've had men ask me for some 'medicine' for their condition; some personalized plan that will work for *them*. This sentiment is exactly what makes PUAs and manosphere 'self-help' speakers sell DVDs and seats at seminars. They claim to have the cure. I say that's bullshit.

I'm not in the business of cures, I'm in the business of connecting dots. Imagine any PUA guru attempting to force fit their plans to accommodate that same 60 year old man's situation. There are various self-styled 'marriage coaches' who make earnest attempts to remedy married men's (lack of) sex lives, but what's the real success rate? Is it even measurable? Even these outlines are just a map, a diagnosis, that men have to subjectively modify for themselves per their own experience, station in life and demographic.

You see, *your* cure, *your* plan of action isn't what any other man's will be, or your future son's, or anyone else reading my work. I can give you a map, but you still have to make your own trail. I'm not your doctor, I want you to be your doctor.

What I experience day to day isn't at all what a majority of men experience. My sexual past, my 'notch count', my 18 year marriage, and what I do professionally sets me apart in a way that I sometimes don't appreciate or take into consideration when I'm advising men.

It's very humbling and affirming when I receive emails or comments from men living in countries I've only seen in pictures who nevertheless share a common male experience that reinforces many of the things I write about – but even within that commonality, I have to remember, my circumstance is not theirs.

I used to walk through a casino almost every day and I'd see the same people. Not the fun glamour you see in commercials or ads about Las Vegas, but the *real* people, the overweight, the housekeeping and table crews, the geriatric spending their savings and social security on a hope they'll win something significant, the desperate and the people just looking for a distraction.

I walk by some of these men and think "how is Game going to help a guy like that?" While I do believe that Game is universally beneficial on many levels (primarily between the sexes, but not exclusively) there's a point where that improvement is going to be limited by a guy's circumstance, where he is in life and what he's made of it so far. It's a manosphere cliché now, but most men aren't ready for the Red Pill. The Red Pill awareness is simply too much for them to accept within the context of their circumstances.

That circumstance isn't based on age or a particular demographic, but Game and a Red Pill perspective is only going to be as liberating for a man in so far as he's willing to accept it in terms of his own circumstance.

Game gets a lot of misconstrued criticism in that ignorant critics presume Game only ever equals sex-starved PUAs in funny hats and "those guys are solely interested in fucking as many low self-esteem sluts as humanly possible."

It's much more difficult and self-examining for them to confront that Game is far more than this, and applicable within relationships, in the workplace (with women and men) and even in their family dealings.

That's kind of a scary prospect for men who're comfortable in living within their own contexts and circumstance. Sport fucking isn't what most men think it is because they've never experienced anything beyond serial monogamy, nor is it what most (Beta) men even have the capacity to actualize for themselves. But, as Game has evolved, it isn't just about spinning plates, or sport fucking, it's more encompassing than this.

Game *is*, or should be, for the everyman.

"He only wants me for sex" or "I need to be sure he's interested in me and not just sex" are the admonishments of women who really have no introspective interest in how a majority of men really approach becoming intimate with women. Oh, it makes for a good rationale when women finally "want to get things right" with a provider, but even the excuse belies a lack of how most men organize their lives to accommodate women's schedules of mating.

Mostly to their detriment, the vast majority of men follow a deductive, but anti-seductive, Beta Game plan of comfort, identification, familiarity and patience with women in the hopes that what they hear women tell them is the way to their intimacy will eventually pan out for them. Their Beta Game plan is in fact to prove they "aren't just in it for the sex" in order to get to a point of having sex with a particular woman.

I always find it ironic when men tell me that their deductive plan for getting after it with a woman is to prove he's not actually trying to get after it with her.

However, this is what most men's Game amounts to; deductively attempting to move into a long term monogamy based on what women, saturated in a presumption of gender equalism, tell him he ought to expect from *himself* in order to align himself with her intimate interest.

I could use the term "appeasement", but that's not what most men want to call it. Most men call it being a better man (for her), better than those *"other guys"* who wont align themselves accordingly. It becomes their point of pride in fact.

Most men, average men – and I don't mean that in a derogatory sense – want a form of security. Most men are designed, perhaps bred, to be necessitous.

To be sure, men need to be constant performers, and constant qualifiers, in order to mitigate Hypergamy. In the past, and to an extent now, this performance simply became a part of who he was as a man and didn't require a constant effort, but increasingly, as male feminization has spread, men have been made to feel necessitous of security.

The security average men seek is rooted in a need for certainty in his ability to meet with a woman's performance standards – and ultimately avoid feminine rejection.

In today's feminine-centric social order, men are ceaselessly bombarded with masculine ridicule, ceaselessly reminded of their inadequacies, and rigorously conditioned to question and doubt any notion of how masculinity *should* be defined – in fact ridicule is the first response for any man attempting to objectively define it.

It's this doubt, this constant reconsideration of his own adequacy to meet the shifting nature of women's hypergamic drive, from which stems this need for security. The average man needs the certainty of knowing that he meets and exceeds a woman's prerequisites in a social circumstance that constantly tells him he never will – and his just asking himself the question if he ever will makes him that much less of a man.

The average man will look for, or create his own rationales to salve this necessitousness. He'll create his own ego in the image of what he thinks he embodies best as being "Alpha" or he'll adopt the easy doctrines of equalism which tell him women and men are fundamentally the same rational actors.

He'll convince himself he's not subject to the capricious whims of feminine Hypergamy or some thematic schedule of women's life events because men and women are more 'evolved' than that– but that nagging doubt will manifest itself when the right circumstances and right opportunities present themselves at the correct time, and just enough to make him think twice about that time line.

Changing Your Programming

I mentioned in the first book that I am not a motivational speaker.

I'm not anyone's savior and I would rather men be their own self-sustaining solutions to becoming the men *they* want and need to be – not a Rollo Tomassi success story, but their own success stories.

That said, let me also add that I would not be writing what I do if I thought that biological determinism, circumstance and social conditioning were insurmountable factors in any Man's life. Men can accomplish great things through acts of will and determination. God willing, they can be masters of those circumstances and most importantly masters of themselves.

With a healthy understanding, respect and awareness of what influences his own condition, a Man can overcome and thrive within the context of them – but he must first be aware of, and accepting of, the conditions in which he operates and maneuvers.

You may not be able to control the actions of others, you may not be able to account for women's Hypergamy, but you can be prepared for them, you can protect yourself from the consequences of them and you can be ready to make educated decisions of your own based upon that knowledge.

You can unplug.

You can change your programming, and you can live a better life no matter your demographic, age, past regrets or present circumstances.

– Rollo Tomassi

APPENDIX

After publishing *The Rational Male* I received a lot of requests for resources, references and blogs men (and women) could find out more about the manosphere.

It's kind of hard to define exactly what constitutes the manosphere since it's so decentralized. Mainstream media like to mischaracterize it as some dangerous fringe collective of misogynist assholes who want to return to 1950's style Patriarchy any time someone they can't ignore does something newsworthy. Those distortion come from a need for easily digestible news-bites, but what confounds them is really the breadth of what the manosphere has come to encompass.

The "manosphere", for lack of a better term, is a very broad consortium of blogs, forums and men's issues sites dedicated to questioning and challenging the ideals of feminine social primacy while raising awareness of how the social changes initiated by those ideals adversely affect men. Needless to say the application of those ideals can get pretty specific to each man's circumstance.

However, the manosphere also encompasess Red Pill / Game and PUA theory and practice resources with the more direct purpose of educating men about the social and psychological influences they find themselves subjected to in contemporary society.

I've described Game thusly: At its root level Game is a series of behavioral modifications to life skills based on psychological and sociological principles to facilitate intersexual relations between genders. I realize that's a mouthful, but it's important to make a distinction between Red Pill theory and Game practice. In my estimation Game is applied Red Pill awareness.

It's also my position that men need a foundational Red Pill awareness of the conditions they're subjected to in a feminine-primary social order, as well as how the psychological and biological underpinnings of male-female relations influence that social order and men themselves.

There's a lot to sift through in the manosphere, and the risk becomes one of men being bogged down in specific issues that agree with their own ego-investments or appear to salve a particular hurt they may have. As I mention in the *Revenge* section of this book, fixating on that desire to even the score or launching a personal crusade against one solitary aspect of the Feminine Imperative often has the affect of retarding a man's real Red Pill awareness and development.

With this in mind I'm going to detail a few of the online resources I think best define a Red Pill perspective. I endorse these sites, but also bear in mind that everyone of them has their own niche, and their own pros and cons.

The Rational Male
http://therationalmale.com/
Of course I'll begin with my own blog. If you're reading this book you've probably got an idea of the content I publish. Many of the essays you've just read are (edited and abridged) versions of my blog posts. I like to stay as objective as possible, knowing that's not really possible, but (to my knowledge) I run the only truly unmoderated comment forum in the manosphere.

If I have a mission statement it's that the only way an idea's strengths and merit can be proven is in the crucible of an open discourse. This is what I make efforts to provide at The Rational Male.

RooshV
http://rooshv.com
I quote Roosh often enough because his insights and experience with the female psyche are among the most accurate in the manosphere. In fact you can't really mention the manosphere proper without recognizing Roosh's contributions to it. His fingerprints are literally on everything.

Roosh is nominally a PUA due to his decade long treks through South America, Northern and Eastern Europe and discovering the cultural particulars of the dating and mating environments in the countries he visits. In some circles this and his outspokenness has earned him a less than shinning reputation in the mainstream, but from a Red Pill perspective his related experiences are invaluable.

Chateau Heartiste – Roissy
http://heartiste.wordpress.com
Roissy, the original proprietor of what is now Chateau Heartiste, is the inarguable godfather of the modern manosphere. His revelations on Game and the psycho-social underpinnings of why Game works have formed the encyclopedic backbone of Red Pill awareness for a decade.

He and his collective of bloggers aren't the most accessible, and at times can be socially and politically sidetracked, but his early essays are the go-to reference points for every current manosphere blogger. There is no more prolific a Red Pill writer than Roissy.

The Red Pill – subreddit
http://reddit.com/r/TheRedPill/

The Red Pill subreddit (TRP) is fast approaching 100,000 subscribers at the time of my writing this and with good reason; it's easily the best warehouse of Red Pill discussion on the net. It's well moderated to stay focused on the Red Pill / Game topics as well as current affairs that affect and influence Red Pill awareness and application.

I can't praise this forum enough. In just a short time TRP has become a hub of Red Pill thought and it's not limited to PUA techniques, but covers a wide variety of Red Pill outreach and subdomains (married men Red Pill, etc.). It's fast popularity is a strong indication of the growth of this awareness is taking.

Dalrock
https://dalrock.wordpress.com/
Thoughts from a happily married father on a post feminist world.

I don't specifically focus on religious topics on The Rational Male unless some aspect of religion is directly related to Red Pill relevant intersexual relations. That, and because if I did it would probably come very close to reading like what Dalrock has been making available for over five years on his own blog now.

If you have religious reservations about the 'morality' of the Red Pill Dalrock is the best at handling that awareness in a religious context. His blog is the best of what I call the Christo-Manosphere. He's also a consummate, well researched statistician with regard to modern marriage and divorce trends and their social implications. I highly recommend him to any Christian who discovers the Red Pill.

The SoSuave Discussion Forum
http://www.sosuave.net/forum/index.php

The SoSuave forum was the incubator of my earliest Red Pill ideas. I owe most of my own formal awarness to the years of discussion on the Mature Men's board. While I am still a moderator on this board, my participation since launching my blog has declined. However, if you're interested in reading some of my earliest Red Pill ideas just do a basic member name search for "Rollo Tomassi" and you can see the archives of how it all began.

That said, SoSuave continues to be a melting pot of Red Pill, Game, and men's issues discussion. Also, if you're a teenage guy who's just discovered this book, the *High School* forum on SoSuave is a good resource for you.

GLOSSARY

One aspect of the Red Pill / Game intersexual awareness community that tends to confuse men who first discover it is the terminology and acronyms we use. I've made an attempt to include the long versions of these acronyms in this book's content, but that still doesn't account for much of the jingoisms the larger community uses.

I'm going to present a glossary of terms here, but it's important to understand that, for better or worse, these terms are relative placeholders for more abstract ideas. Even "The Red Pill" is a poor substitute for an ideological awareness of the real nature and interplay of intergender relations, but it works as a relative name for that awareness. We get it when we think about relating it to waking up to truth and the 'red pill' moment from *The Matrix* movie serves as a usable association.

Well before the inception of my blog, in the early beginnings of what would evolve into the manosphere, there was a need of terminology to describe the more abstract concepts developing in the 'community'. Some of these analogies and terms are still with the manosphere today, others have morphed into more useful abstractions; Alpha Widows, Hypergamy (in its true nature), the Feminine Imperative, even Game are all examples of established terms or analogies for understood abstractions. Among these are also the concepts of a man being Alpha and Beta.

Alpha & Beta

I'm not including these two terms in the glossary because I think the content of this and my previous book more than adequately describe *my* definitions of both terms, but I will elaborate on them briefly here.

I need to address the basis of what I believe are the most common misunderstandings about the term Alpha.

One of the most common disconnects men encounter with the Red Pill for the first time is equating the term *Alpha* with its usage in describing the mating habits of Lions, Wolves or Silver Back Gorillas. It's easy to ridicule or simply dismiss a valid, but uncomfortable, Red Pill truth when you're simplistically comfortable in defining '*Alpha Male*' in literal etymological terms.

This is the first resistance Blue Pill men claim they have with the Red Pill. They have no problem understanding and using abstractions for Blue Pill concepts they themselves are ego-invested in, but challenge that belief-paradigm with uncomfortable Red Pill truths and their first resort is to obstinately define Alpha (as well as Hypergamy) in as narrow, binary and literal a sense as they can muster.

The Purple Pill

The next most common misunderstanding comes from conflating the abstractions of Alpha and Beta with masculine and feminine traits. In this (often deliberate) misdirection, the concepts of being Alpha or Beta become synonymous with being masculine or feminine. This is the personal basis of Alpha and Beta many Purple Pill advocates (really blue pill apologists) comfortably redefine for themselves, to suit their identities.

This Purple Pill conflation is really just a comforting return the Curse of Carl Jung – anima & animus – if the complete man is an even mix of Alpha and Beta, masculine and feminine, then all the worst aspects of his "betaness" can't be all bad, and he reinterprets what really amounts to a complete androgyny as "being the *best* balance".

Unfortunately, and as Blue Pill men will later attest, the feminine expects to find its paired balance in the masculine, not an equalist idealization of both in the same man. Thus women, on a limbic level, expect men to be Men.

This one of the missives of an equalitarian mindset; that an individualized, egalitarian balance of masculine and feminine aspects in two independent people should replace the natural complementary interdependence of masculine and feminine attributes in a paired balance that humans evolved into.

What Purple Pill temperance really equates to is a 21st century return to the 20th century feminized meme "men need to get in touch with their feminine sides"… or else risk feminine rejection. 60+ years of post sexual revolution social engineering has put the lie to what an abject failure this concept has been.

What they fail to grasp is that an Alpha mindset is not *definitively* associated with masculine attributes. There are plenty of high-functioning, masculine men we would characterize as Alpha based on our perception of them in many aspects of life, who nonetheless are abject supplicating Betas with regard to how they interact with, and defer to women.

Whether that disconnect is due to a learned, Beta deference to the feminine (White Knighting), some internalized fear of rejection, or just a natural predisposition to be so with women, isn't the issue; what matters is that the abstraction of *Alpha* isn't an absolute definitive association with the masculine.

Likewise, Beta attributes are neither inherently feminine. As has been discussed ad infinitum in the manosphere, 80%+ of modern men have been conditioned (or otherwise) to exemplify and promote a feminine-primary, supportive Beta role for themselves and as many other men as they can convince to identify more with the feminine.

The Beta mindset isn't so much one of adopting a feminine mindset as much as it adopts a deference to, and the support of, a feminine-primary worldview.

The reason the advocates of a Purple Pill (watered down Red Pill) ideology want to make the association of Alpha = Masculine, Beta = Feminine is because the "get in touch with your feminine side" Beta attributes they possess in spades can be more easily characterized as "*really*" being Alpha if it helps make them the more androgynously acceptable male they mistakenly believe women are attracted to (if not directly aroused by).

Acronyms and Terms

Many of the terms on this list have had their abstraction described in better detail in the first book, *The Rational Male,* others you can find with a simple search on my blog, but I'm presenting them here for the convenience of newer readers.

Alpha Widow - A woman (usually post wall) who has been previously intimate with an Alpha male. This experience tends to develop into a complex where a woman pines for and compares all her subsequent lovers and / or husband to the Alpha precedent that lover set.

AMOG – Alpha Male Of Group.

AF/BB - Short form for Alpha Fucks/Beta Bucks, the distilled sexual strategy dictated by feminine Hypergamy

AFC - Average Frustrated Chump. (Also known as beta)

ASD - Anti-Slut Defense. A filibuster or delaying action a sexually unsure will employ to rationalize her sexual hesitancy with a suitor.

AWALT - All Women Are Like That.

Blue Pill – From *The Matrix* movie and its sequels. The path of conformity with Society's expectations; the state of being unaware of the problems engendered by a feminine primary social order and an ignorance of intersexual dynamics promoted by it.

Close - The culmination of an interaction. Often preceded by an indication of the type of close, eg. f-close (full close or fuck close, the interaction led to sex), k-close (kiss), #close (receiving phone #).

DT, or Dark Triad - A combination of three personality traits: Narcissism, Machiavellianism, and Psycopathy.

DHV – Display of Higher Value, the evident establishing of anything that improves your sexual market value perception in the eyes of another.

DLV - Display of lower value.

Dread Game - From *The Rational Male*. Purposefully or casually inciting jealousy in an LTR by openly inviting attention from other women. **Soft Dread** is similar, but less open. With Soft Dread, attention is indirect and casual, generated unsolicited from a third party. Creating the possibility of female attention is often enough to generate a dread anxiety. (If you develop a great body, she knows that other women will find that attractive without having to actually see other women displaying interest.) The purpose of using Dread is to get the target (wife, girlfriend, plate) to step up their game to compete with other interested women.

FR - Field Report.

Frame - The psychological context in which an interpersonal dynamic is perceived. Maintaining frame is often cited as the most important aspect of Alpha behavior. See Iron Rule of Tomassi #1 in *The Rational Male*

Game – Game is a series of behavioral modifications to life skills based on psychological and sociological principles to facilitate intersexual relations between genders.

Hamster - Colloquialism used to describe the way women rationalization to resolve mental incongruity and avoid cognitive dissonance. The core mechanism that allows women to say one thing and do a different thing.

HB - Hot Babe (often followed by a number as an indication of ranking on a 1-10 scale).

Incel - Involuntarily Celibate. A man who wants to get laid, but can't.

IOI - Indication of Interest.

LDR - Long Distance Relationship

LJBF - Let's Just Be Friends (See Orbiter)

LMR - Last Minute Resistance.

LTR - Long Term Relationship.

Manosphere - The loose collection of blogs, message boards, and other sites run by and/or read by MRAs, MGTOW, PUAs etc and any Red Pill associated people/groups.

MGTOW – Men Going Their Own Way; the growing contingent of the male population who are declining participation in the modern sexual marketplace.

MRA - Men's Rights activist.

MRM - Men's Rights Movement.

Orbiter - Also known as Beta Orbiter. A Beta man who accepts the proposal to "just be friends" from a girl. He will stick around her and constantly validate her whenever she requests it. Also known as "friendzone." She will keep him around because he will do anything for her and provide validation, giving small hints that he might eventually win her love- but he never will. Typical signs of orbiter status: likes and comments on new facebook photos. Go-to guy when girl has problem with boyfriend. Also known as Emotional Tampon.

Plate - Woman with whom you are in a non-exclusive relationship with. Spinning plates is the act of having multiple non-exclusive relations working simultaneously. Plate Theory can be found in *The Rational Male*.

Preselection - The idea that women are more attracted to men who already have the interest of other women or large societal approval of status. This aids in a woman evaluating a man's SMV by confirming that other women have already judged him favorably.

PUA – Pick-Up Artist.

Shit Test, or Fitness Test - A statement, question or social predicament initiated (subconsciously or deliberately) by a woman to evaluate Alpha reflexive traits in men.

SMV – Sexual Market Value.

SMP - Sexual Market Place.

The Wall - See *The Wall – The Rational Male*. The point in a woman's life where her ego and self-assessed view of her sexual market value exceeds her actual sexual market value; the beginning of true SMV decline. Usually occurs as a wake-up shock to women when they realize that their sexual agency with men was temporary and that their looks are fading. This usually results with first denial and then a sudden change in priority towards looking for a husband. Even after hitting the wall, many women will squander a few more precious years testing her SMV with alphas to double-check, hoping her perceived decline was a fluke, this will make her even more bitter when she finally has to settle for a worse-beta than she could've gotten before because of squandering her youth.

White Knight – See *Enter White Knight – The Rational Male*. (1) a man who "comes to the rescue" of a woman, or of women, reflexively, emotionally-driven, without thought or even looking at the situation; (2) a man in authority who enables the Feminine Imperative by default in his legislative actions, judgments, or rulings, reflexively and emotionally driven, without genuine judicial insight.

Credits

Credit to The Red Pill subreddit for the base definitions.

(pg. 31) Menstrual Cycle Illustration Wikimedia Commons

(pg. 97) Older Americans' Breakups Are Causing A 'Graying' Divorce Trend
February 24, 2014
http://www.npr.org/2014/02/24/282105022/older-americans-are-causing-a-graying-divorce-trend

(pg. 142) Nobody marries their best sex ever – Jennifer Wright, November 25, 2012New York Post
http://nypost.com/2012/11/25/nobody-marries-their-best-sex-ever/

(pg.143) Washington Post – Carolyn Hax, Columnist
http://www.washingtonpost.com/lifestyle/style/carolyn-hax/2014/04/18/898e82ce-b9bb-11e3-9a05-c739f29ccb08_story.html